FINDING AN UNSEEN GOD

M E A N I N G J F E A N H O H
P T S G N A K S C R W I B O T
Z E **F** L X G N O K I O G P X A
R N O **I** T S E U Q U N E V S P
J O U R **N** E Y L N Q D B M C L
E I T F N **D** E O N N E T S I L
G T C R B A **I** A K I R W F A S
D R A P A S M **N** A H Y E P S T
E U F B U E I H **G** T H K E C L
L T A L E H H M I L C **AN** I H
W H L R T D N L V A R O N E D
O I E C P F A I T H A G T N P
N **UNSEEN** J A F E S I C B
K Q I N R **GOD** W P S M K E H

REFLECTIONS OF A FORMER ATHEIST

ALICIA BRITT CHOLE

BETHANYHOUSE
MINNEAPOLIS, MINNESOTA

Published by Bethany House Publishers
11400 Hampshire Avenue South
Bloomington, Minnesota 55438

Bethany House Publishers is a division of
Baker Publishing Group, Grand Rapids, Michigan.

Printed in the United States of America

Library of Congress Cataloging-in-Publication Data
Chole, Alicia Britt.
    Finding an unseen god : reflections of a former atheist / Alicia Britt Chole.
        p. cm.
    Includes bibliographical references.
    Summary: "Presents the author's personal journey from atheism to Christianity. Examines the mysteries of life and faith, including how different religious belief system influence a person. Intended for atheists, agnostics, and theists"—Provided by publisher.
    ISBN 978-0-7642-0602-3 (pbk. : alk. paper) 1. Chole, Alicia Britt. 2. Christian converts—United States—Biography. 3. Atheism. 4. Faith. I. Title.

BV4935.C46A3 2009
248. 2'46092—dc22
[B]
                                                                        2009005410

to my dad

thank you for asking me penetrating questions
thank you for teaching me to dunk Oreos in milk
i ache to hear your voice again

the daughter

CHAPTER

CONTENTS

C
H
A
P
T
CONT**E**NTS
R

CONTENTS

C
H
A
P
T
E
R

```
M E A N I N G J F E A N H O H
P T S G N A K S C R W I B O T
Z E F L X G N O K I O G P X A
R N O I T S E U Q U N E V S P
J O U R N E Y L N Q D B M C L
E I T F N D E O N N E T S I L
G T C R B A I A K I R W F A S
D R A P A S M N A H Y E P S T
E U F B U E I H G T H K E C L
L T A L E H H M I L C A N I H
W H L R T D N L V A R O N E D
O I E C P F A I T H A G T N P
N U N S E E N J A F E S I C B
K Q I N R G O D W P S M K E H
```

ANGST	JOURNEY	QUESTION
ASK	KNOWLEDGE	REALITY
BEGIN	LIFE	SCIENCE
DEBATE	LISTEN	SEARCH
FAITH	MEANING	SOUL
HEART	MIND	THINK
HOPE	NAME	TRUTH
ILLUSION	PAIN	WONDER
INQUIRE	PATH	

See solution on page 174

ON THE DOORSTEP SHATTERED

Truth was dead.

God had never lived.

Life was filled with pain.

And death was the end of life.

These beliefs formed my worldview as a young woman: I sincerely believed that there was no God. God had not created man. Man had obviously created God.

Most of life's truly painful problems were never going to be answered by science, reason, or experience. So it was understandable that individuals and entire cultures would create mythical beings—call it God or call them gods—to fill in the gaps and calm their fears. As a young Atheist, I simply considered myself a realist who preferred unanswered questions over fairy tales.

That was the end of the matter, at least in the beginning. Over the years, I transitioned from quiet confidence in my choice to a vocal critiquing of others' choices. I found it perplexing that intelligent humans would engage in the self-deception required to birth and feed faith. Observing people fabricate (or inherit) a culturally customized version of a supreme being, assign deity to their construct, and then claim that their invention gave them "peace" was disturbing for sure, but not devastating.

After all, everyone had coping mechanisms for living. Some buried themselves in work or a cause. Some turned to drugs or drink. Some focused on fitness or fixated on chocolate, and some consoled themselves by hoping for a better afterlife or deferring to a benevolent designer. All were attempts at managing the unresolved.

As an emerging adult, however, my Atheism gained momentum and developed a less tolerant edge. Faith did seem to empower some to be more optimistic, but what did it matter if it was not based in reality? I would rather be sober than sappy; discouraged than in denial.

Look around.

Innocent children are being abused globally in record numbers. Some will never know healthy love. And the religious claim that there is a godlike being that holds power over the affairs of mankind? Try telling *that* to the children: "I'm sorry that the vilest of beings bearing the name human are committing atrocities at your expense. But be encouraged, God lives and he loves you!" Please. Self-medicate on religion if you must. But do not offer it to me or the less fortunate in this world as some cruel placebo for unexplainable pain and unabated injustice.

Then one day, without warning and without invitation, my Atheistic worldview was shattered like fine glassware on a concrete floor, leaving me bloodied, stunned, and speechless. It was as though something you were absolutely certain existed only as the stuff and fluff of fairy tales knocked loud and clear and then stood there offending all your senses on the doorstep.

But perhaps it would be helpful to rewind the journey a decade or two, and start a thread closer to the beginning.

1

UPK
  ALH   WK
UNSINKABLE
  JOYDFL
    IRDOCTOR
   CHOICE
     DN
      L

"This is going to be hard to hear. I think you should consider terminating the pregnancy."[1]

Angie was stunned. "Why?!" she demanded, gripping Lou's hand.

"Your Rh factors are incompatible. Angie, your blood is Rh-negative. Lou's is Rh-positive. If your baby inherits Lou's Rh factor, you could develop antibodies that cross the placenta and attack the baby's blood."

The weighty words were an unexpected assault on the happiest season Angie had ever known. Months earlier, when Lou expressed his concern that she seemed sad, Angie surprised both of them with a flood of tears and an agonizing cry of "I want a baby!" Angie knew she was pregnant well before the tests made it official. Her joy was unsinkable.

The doctor continued, "Your baby will most likely suffer brain damage and perhaps be physically deformed. He or she will need a transfusion at birth and you may lose your life in the delivery room. I'm sorry to have to give you such news. This is why people have blood tests before they get married. You should have never conceived a child together."

Roe v. Wade was still eight years away from that cool spring day in Las Vegas, Nevada. But the doctor knew that a woman's life was at stake. In his professional opinion, terminating the pregnancy was the most reasonable medical option he knew to propose.

"It's your choice, Angie," Lou offered.

Angie's mind was fixed. With anger disproportionate to her small size, she answered: "This baby is ours. I don't care what it looks like. I don't care what it can or can't do. I'm carrying my baby!"

R
SI ACN
SUDDENLYME J
VNHERTC
UNHEARDP
WOT
F **AWAKE**
T

The natural rush of breathing crisp, fresh, morning mountain air. The cool clarity of wading in pure, green island waters. The creative anticipation that arises from savoring a cup of organic peppermint tea.

I can only offer images in my attempt to capture the hours and days immediately following the encounter. In a period of minutes, I had abruptly transitioned from being completely certain that god-concepts were self-medicating illusions of the masses to being confronted mentally, physically, and emotionally by tangible confirmation that God *is*.

Not remodeled or restored. I felt *new*; suddenly alert and awake in a way I had never before experienced, as though life—true life— had taken its first deep breath.

Stunned by the encounter, it took me some time to readjust

to the presence of others in the room. Turning to my friend Susie and her mom, I saw tears falling from faces that were more serious than celebratory. Quietly, we walked together by the pastor, who said softly, "You do realize that something has just happened to you." I nodded but was still too overwhelmed to speak.

Taking a few steps down the center (and only) aisle, I exited the small building and walked on chalky white gravel toward the car when someone called to me. "I have a word from God for you," a man said, running to catch up. Turning around I thought, *A what from whom?* Then he spoke:

> Trust in the Lord with all your heart and lean not on your own understanding; in all your ways acknowledge him, and he will make your paths straight.[2]

"Okay," I replied, without the faintest idea of what these words would mean to me in the days to come. We drove back to the house in silence.

Thirteen years later, my husband and I found the little white building on a drive through Illinois. Knocking on the door, a man answered and immediately recognized me. "People still talk about that day," he explained. "It meant more to them than you could know." Ushering us inside, he walked over to a file cabinet and pulled out a few stapled pages. "This is the message I spoke that day. You can have it if you'd like," the pastor offered. Having never heard it the first time, I was now grateful for the opportunity to read it. "Thank you," I said. Then, unheard message in hand, I walked into the room where the encounter had occurred.

The room's simplicity was soothing. Wood pews, fading carpet, four walls. This was my sanctuary. Stillness was my offering.

Back in the foyer, Barry learned about the history of the little white building. The church had been in trouble that sacred day so long ago. People were hurting, some had left, and others were leaving. Shortly afterward a painful migration would scatter the members to other places. Later, the little white building would open its doors again with a new name. Though no longer standing beside one another week after week, the faithful were still united in spirit by their memories, one of which was the day their God interrupted the life of an unsuspecting young Atheist.

2

```
  C   Z A
MO NOT G
  SOHBLUE PKOL
  BABY PS
TUQKHN I   D
    ABWONDER
VEGASK Y
        W
        I
```

Lou and Angie left the doctor's office that day and never looked back on their choice. Weeks later, when the doctor called to let them know their baby was a boy, they began buying everything blue. Louis Allen—the name they gave their anxiously awaited son—would be born to parents who wanted him desperately; to a mom who was willing to die so that he could live.

In his earnest and educated prognoses, the doctor had been right—but only about one thing.

The Sheet Metal Workers Union was still on strike October 29, 1965, when Angie checked into the hospital. Lou had found much-needed work in Utah, but when he heard that Angie had gone into labor, he chose to leave (and lose) the job and drive back home to Las Vegas. Two new grandmothers phoned while he was rushing through a shower to get to the hospital: "Tell Lou the baby's here and it's a . . ."

Angie lay unconscious in intensive care when Lou arrived. As the doctor had predicted, she almost died giving birth. Six days later, Angie would be released from the hospital, but it would be four months of bed rest before she would be strong enough to hold her baby.

The unneeded transfusion cart had already been rolled away when the nurse placed a perfectly healthy baby in Lou's arms. It was love at first sight. "What's the baby's name?" the waiting nurse asked, pen in hand. The pink cap confirmed the phone call: A new name was needed. "Her name is Alicia, named after Angie's mom," Lou replied. "Alicia Lynn Britt."

Lost in the wonder of holding his dreamed-for girl, Lou had no idea that the name he had chosen for her meant "truthful one."[3]

P

THEO**DAYS**G

Y BH**FU** P

ESMR **TWA**LL

WD I **THE**QC OB

CUR **R**EHSK

AC I TNJE

L **ENCOUNTER**FLO I

L

B

The encounter occurred on June 26, 1983. That date marks my life like the dismantling of the Berlin Wall marks Germany. This was more than symbolic. This was physical. A new era had commenced.

Several memories stand out from the next few days: my ever-loving parents' panic, the Bowheads' utter disbelief, and a deep personal ache for two things I had previously never even remotely desired.

(The full story of the Bowheads will unfold in the alternating thread. For now, though, it is enough to know that the Bowheads were two young women who dared to befriend an angry Atheist.)

Returning to Susie's home that day, I picked up the phone and gushed to my parents about the encounter. These are the parents who stood by supportively while their daughter enthusiastically began, excelled in, and eventually quit ballet, tap, jazz, piano, Spanish, drama, speech, and golf. This was the mother who worked primarily to give her only child braces, every acne treatment known to man, a college education, and the opportunity to explore any hobby or interest that she desired. This was the father who cheered his daughter on in her every pursuit while privately pondering why nothing held her interest.

These were the parents who listened politely that day, said "Okay, honey. We'll talk more about this when you get home," then proceeded to page through a phone book and call the psychologist. Dad and Mom were extremely worried that perhaps I had experienced a breakdown or been drugged. Creepy cults abounded in the '70s and '80s, and Dad's first concern was to make sure that his baby was safe and had not fallen in with fruitcakes.

That's weird, I mused after the call. *Oh well, they probably were just distracted. I'll call the Bowheads!*

"Shawny! You'll never guess what just happened!"

"What's his name?" she asked with a smile in her voice.

"His name? Jesus! I just met God."

(Silence)

"Did you hear me? I just met Jesus!"

Shawny made no response, so I kept going. Finally, when I took a breath, Shawny let me know that she did not believe me and did not appreciate my new attempt at mocking her faith.

(Click)

24

The Bowheads did eventually believe me. Shawny said she knew I was telling the truth as soon as she saw my face.

Having exhausted my calling circle, I asked Susie and her mom if we could go to the bookstore as soon as possible. I had an urgent craving for two things. The second thing was music: I wanted to hear music with lyrics about God. Susie's mom had a cassette (do not laugh, this was a BIG step up from the 8-tracks) that I wanted to buy. Sitting in front of their tape recorder, I would press Rewind and Play, Rewind and Play, Rewind and Play . . . the words captivated me.

> Open our eyes Lord
> We want to see Jesus
> To reach out and touch Him
> And say that we love Him
> Open our ears Lord
> And help us to listen
> Open our eyes Lord
> We want to see Jesus* [4]

So we drove to the mall's bookstore where I purchased a cassette of Amy Grant's *My Father's Eyes* (they were out of the cassette I was looking for) as well as the first thing I was craving. The cassette was enjoyed and then given away long ago, but the first thing is still in my possession. It is weathered, torn, and bears the stains and warps of multiple spills. It is coming apart, exudes a distinct odor, and years ago contracted bugs. It is treasured and I will not part with it barring a fire: my very first Bible.

*All rights reserved. Used by permission.

3

STRANGE
BUT LOW
MAINTENANCE

Not "Mama" or "Dada," my parents teased me that the first word out of my mouth was "WHY?" Evidently I have been asking questions since I could speak (and not much has changed).

My cheerleader for life, glorious Mom described me as a "perfect" child who never threw a tantrum or climbed the walls . . . who crawled backward but never forward and who was potty trained at birth. Yes, I too remain skeptical.

According to my parents' reports, I simply sat and read books or sat and played the piano or sat and watched Johnny Carson with my dad over a tall glass of milk and Oreos. Those were simpler days when Oreos were just Oreos, no Double Stuf, no peanut butter filling . . . just pure, original, Oreo goodness.

My favorite room in the house was the bathroom. The enclosed bathroom is a gift from heaven for all true introverts. Bathrooms give you full, unquestioned freedom to be blissfully antisocial. Turn on the lights, close the door, pick up a book or magazine, and a simple bathroom is transformed into a private library: *Webster's Dictionary, Reader's Digest, National Geographic,* and *Nancy Drew* mysteries were my favorite reads.

Even today, when my family cannot find me, they head to the bathroom. Why? Because decades later I still am sitting and thinking. The *Digest* has been replaced by Japanese number puzzles, and Nancy Drew gave way long ago to healthy living newsletters and business theory books. But through the years Webster's and *National Geographic* have maintained their favored status—it is hard to beat an unabridged dictionary and exceptional photojournalism.

Now that I have children of my own, though, I understand that "perfect" is actually parental code for "strange but low-maintenance." What child just sits and thinks all day? Yet according to my parents, I was quite content to spend hours learning and processing my perceptions of life in the sanctuary of my mind.

```
      W A L I V E
 B THUS D    O H
 N A K  SAYS I
S K R T E J I M I N Y L C
      Z CRICKET
 H U N G E R L J
      F P S
```

If someone based their views, choices, and values upon a source that you perceived to be inaccurate at best and misleading at worst, they would not gain ground with you by quoting that source. I understand. For me as an Atheist, when people referred to the Bible they gained about as much ground as if they had referenced Jiminy Cricket, Pinocchio's fairy-tale conscience. In other words, they lost ground every time they said, "It is written . . ."

But after the encounter, I possessed an immediate, unexplainable, undeniable hunger to read the Bible. Previously, when the Bowheads had given me those little green Gideon Bibles, I culturally could not bring myself to throw gifts away, so I stacked them in the recesses of my bathroom. Every once in a while after I had read and reread the most current issue of *National Geographic*, the back of my shampoo bottle, and the bottom of the Kleenex box, out of sheer boredom I would reach for one of those little green books.

Flipping through the onionskin pages, I scanned the tiny King James print and saw *nothing*. Not that the pages were blank. The very words were insubstantial to me. They felt even thinner than the paper they were printed upon. Letter after letter and line upon line passed through my eye gate, ran into my mind, and slid off.

Do you remember the last time you stared in vain at a text written in an unknown language? That is how it felt. Words, sentences, paragraphs, and chapters were evident, but meaning eluded me. The words did not stick to me. It felt like I was reading static.

"What nonsense," I would moan and toss the gift aside.

However, after that day in June 1983, when God suddenly *was*, I ached for a Bible. I thirsted for one like I thirsted for water. When I held one—how can I say this—it was *alive*. The Bible was no longer a book; it was a *voice*. I could not hear it or read it fast enough. So I read, and read, and read, and read, not to learn what I was supposed to do or what I was supposed to believe, but to discover Who this Presence was that had interrupted my existence. Did I understand all of it? No. But I was not reading to teach; I was reading because I had to hear—I had to experience—the *voice*.

That blue study Bible was the first thing I packed when I drove off to start college a few weeks after the encounter. I read it voraciously: in the morning, in between classes, and when I was supposed to be studying. And I distinctly recall the first time someone asked, "Why are you reading that? Don't you know it's full of inconsistencies?" I felt startled, as though a stranger had interrupted a phenomenal meal-of-a-lifetime to ask me if I had checked the chef's credentials. "Pardon?" I replied, revealing my parents' Southern roots. "Inconsistencies? Can you show me one?" That particular individual could not, but his challenge had raised a valid question that I frankly had been too delighted and captivated to yet consider on this side of belief: Is the Bible reliable?

4

F L W
AR N   V A S K
    I M E M O R I E S
    E B **P A T I E N T**
T N   X **C O A C H**
P D A D G   Z I M
    S

One of my earliest vivid memories was that moment we all experience as small children when we suddenly become aware that people's lives continue even when they are not in our presence. Some visitor left, and I recall watching the door close and realizing that they were off to live a life I could not see.

From that point onward, I would just stare in awe at the people I had to walk past—they had whole lives that would never intersect visibly with mine. Cemeteries were entirely overwhelming: to think that people were born, contributed—for better or for worse—to life, and died and all that remained to mark their entire existence for the passing stranger was some stone in the ground etched with fading letters . . .

Life's fragility astounded me. Day after day I would observe it as carefully as I could, and then bounce any conclusions, concerns, and questions off of my brilliant dad.

"Whatcha thinking, daughter?" he would prompt with a sparkle in his light brown eyes. A gifted listener, Dad would wait attentively and then ask challenging follow-up questions, all the while patiently coaching me to identify the *why* beneath the *what* of my thoughts, to critique perceptions, and to welcome disagreement.

Like old friends, Dad and I would sit together into the wee hours, laughing at Johnny's jokes (Why is it that his face always reminded me of a happy chipmunk?), smirking through the oh-so-unpredictable dialogue of *Star Trek*, and talking until we could not keep our eyes open.

There, in those late-night talks, I had my first glimpse of the Divine. Not that Dad believed in a god or gods, not at all. But Dad let me know that no question was foolish, no subject was off limits. Nothing shocked him, shamed him, or shut him down . . . and *that* is truly godlike.

48

PEF   TNP
LC**THE**RSLE
H NSE A
RANCIENTT
VOICENOM
FDWZ
S

Have you ever stopped to ask if Plato really wrote *Republic*?

How do we determine that any text is reliable? How do we know that *Republic* was not written by some guy named Moe? Or why do we not wonder if a sneaky scribe twisted Plato's words to reflect his own philosophy of government? After all, Plato lived over two thousand years ago, and the *Republic* that we read is not Plato's original manuscript or even a copy of a copy of the original. Our oldest copy of *Republic* has been dated at AD 900, which separates it from Plato's actual pen by thirteen hundred years.

As a college student with a passion for research, it made sense to me that the Bible should be subject to whatever process any ancient manuscript underwent to have its authenticity verified. I began my quest by first asking people what their concerns were about the Bible: What and where were these "inconsistencies"? Second, I tried to learn how scholars determined the authenticity of ancient manuscripts. Third, I read a book called *Evidence That Demands A Verdict* by Josh McDowell. In other words, I did not hesitate to critique the Bible. Why should I be afraid of discovering the truth?

Long story short, I concluded that if I did not question the textual purity of Plato's *Republic* or Caesar's *The Gallic Wars*, it would be inconsistent of me—no, that is not strong enough—it would be hypocritical of me to question the textual purity of the Bible.

And was that the end of the matter? Of course not. Textual purity is one thing, divine inspiration is another. Could the Bible be a faithful reproduction of the writings of honest, historically accurate men who sincerely thought they were hearing from God but who were actually suffering from a shared delusion (i.e., that there was a God to hear from) that happened to span millennia?

You are going to have to answer that question for yourself. Personally, I have revisited the question every four to five years since my days as an undergraduate. To date, I come up with the same answer: I do not think so. The deluded do not live or die like these writers lived and died. But the most compelling evidence I still return to is the *voice*. I have read books that encouraged me, instructed me, even inspired me. I have read books that have brought me to tears and motivated me to action. But this book, this Bible, actually *renews* me. My spirit experiences sustainable, fresh life whenever I hear its *voice*.

Now, there are whole sentences in the Bible that I have since wished some scribe *had* deleted. There are stories that offend my sense of justice and have caused me to struggle with God's character. So when I refer to the Bible, please know that I do not view it as some sort of oasis of peace and joy. The *voice* renews me, but the words sometimes confound me. Biblical writers addressed difficult themes and recounted painful events. Evidently, they felt inspired to leave in parts that on my own I would have felt inclined to leave out. Though uncomfortable, this very honesty is also strangely confidence-inspiring. It makes the book untamed and raw, which reads more like real life.

DAD TE ST
K **AND** C **H I S** OT L V
P J **B I G** P
O D R E A M S T
T A L K **TOE** J R E
Y E

Dad was an entrepreneurial spirit whose life could not stretch long enough to explore all his ideas or fulfill all his dreams. Though my eyes start to sting at the memory, I can still see him in his check-ered blue cotton robe, resting in his favorite recliner, absorbing the stillness of the morning. Freshly brewed coffee in one of his many golf-motif mugs sat steaming as his faithful companion.

As a child I would tiptoe out of my room to the comfort of seeing Dad's silhouette in the darkness. Two signs gave the signal that he was wakeful: the silky trail of his ever-lit cigarette and his in-perpetual-motion right foot. For years I thought Dad just had a hyperactive big toe until he let me in on his secret. His toe was outlining shapes: the smooth lines of the windowpane, the carv-ings of the TV case (they used to come in rather elaborate wood cases), the curled green leaves of Mom's ivy plants.

There he was thinking, inventing, reminiscing, daydreaming, and later in life, exerting all his mental strength to stay calm as his heart lost the will to keep beating. Dad died on my eldest son's fourth birthday. I was the last person who heard his voice. We talked every day, and May 29, 2001, was no exception. Dad adored his grandson—all of his friends would attest to that. Whatever Jonathan did during the week would be transformed by Dad into a captivating tale for his buddies at the bar to hear over and over and over again.

On that last day, he called to wish Jonathan happy birthday and to tell me about a new heart surgery he was monitoring with interest. "I think I might consider that in a year or two after they've worked all the bugs out," he said. Then in closing, "I love you, daughter." "I love you too, Daddy. Talk to you tomorrow." Around thirty minutes later, my dad's enormous heart stopped beating for good.

47

DOZMR
UTG EHBC
UBKEV**AUSTIN**
JFUSION
MWIRYX
DE

With my brand-new blue Bible in hand, I flew home a few days after the encounter to resume my summer schedule of daytimes at Padre Island and nighttimes in Mexico. My dear parents watched with stunned bewilderment as their daughter returned to her old life with a new faith. The fusion was messy.

Susie's grandmother connected me to a lively church, and as the weeks passed I wanted to be there more than anywhere else. I savored everything: the teaching, the singing, the small groups. When not at a service, I was jabbering joyfully about God's surprising existence to my parents at home, peers at the beach, and inebriated band members at the bar.

All the while, my parents' alarm was mounting. *Surely this too will pass,* they thought with sincere concern. History gave them reason to hope. A liberal arts girl well before college, I was disciplined as a student, dedicated to learning, and disinterested in confining myself to one person or one pursuit.

"No. Nothing and no one has ever held her interest for long. Yet," my parents added with caution, "doesn't it seem like she's glowing?"

Above all, Dad and Mom were committed to my happiness. Though they were worried, my joy was undeniable. So they positioned themselves to catch me when the bottom fell out of my newfound faith. It would be years before they, in peace, finally felt the freedom to abandon that post. In between, my parents trusted that college would bring me back to my senses.

In 1983, the University of Texas in Austin was one of the largest colleges in the country, with enrollment hovering around fifty thousand. My program, however, was small, intimate, and intense. Plan II Pre-law was a dream degree for me. Its liberal arts curriculum and instructional emphases on thinking, researching, writing, and discussion created a rich environment for the evaluation and continued nurture of my growing faith. The professors were substantial, the students were brilliant, and each time I said "I believe . . ." some smart someone would speak up and say, "Why?"

In the morning I would open the blue book and read, "In the beginning God created,"[5] and then walk into biology class to discuss theories of evolution. In the afternoon I would open the blue book and read, "Jesus answered, 'I am the way and the truth and the life,' "[6] and then walk into philosophy class to discuss many ways and many truths in many lives.

Such an environment was an invaluable gift to me. The questions, the challenges, and even the conflicts served to make my growing faith lean and wiry. Looking back, I am extremely grateful for the timing of the encounter. For how my brain is wired, entering faith as an adult, especially as a young college student, possessed many advantages.

First, the encounter was immediately memorable, intellectually undeniable, and interpersonally verifiable (i.e., it had been witnessed by others). Second, not having grown up in this faith, I had very few preconceptions of what followers of Jesus did and did not do. No doubt, more than a few were puzzled by the dissonance between my clearly earnest faith and still-in-formation theology. But the close-to-blank slate gave me the freedom to focus on simply *knowing* God as opposed to worrying about if it *looked like* I knew God. Third, in college I had the privilege of living faith not in the singular, but in the plural. Next to the blue book, nothing was more spiritually formative for me than walking with the community of faith I found in Austin.

6

```
    H
    A
KERHYTHM
  S  CUQIT
RESOLVEDNCO
JONEOQDAD
  PMASTER
   GZ   S
```

When he did not answer her hourly call, Mom rushed home to find Dad motionless, leaning against the wall. His unfinished crossword puzzle sat in his lap with a pencil mark that ran off the page . . . and never came back again. When I received the news, I physically collapsed on the floor, unable to breathe.

Returning home to help Mom make the final arrangements, I sat in Dad's big recliner, stroking the spot where his tapping fingers had worn a hole in the armrest. Poor circulation ended Dad's dancing days way too early, but he always had some rock 'n' roll song playing in his mind while his fingers pounded out the rhythm on the soft leather of his chair.

When I could see enough through the tears, I began searching Dad's computer frantically for some blog or journal or memoir in which he had passed on his history and wisdom. No such luck, and that is a true pity. Dad was a master storyteller, a mesmerizing communicator, a wealth of insight and information. I inherited part of his mind but none of his memory.

Dad remembered every detail of his childhood—even those details he would have preferred to forget. His gambling father abandoned the family when Dad was very small. Growing up in poverty, Dad's father sporadically popped into his life here and there, only long enough to make promises that he would never keep. He made money in Vegas . . . but could not hold on to it long enough to help his only child. He bought Dad a car . . . and never made the payments. Dad was so embarrassed when the bank came to take his car away.

Disappointment and anger meshed into resolve: Dad would never be poor and he would never be an untrustworthy parent. He did his best to achieve those goals to the very, very end.

R
K   W
YE **AMD FACE**
  G I POSEURS
  Z **ON** I **GOD**
  QSA   KH
  CWYJEBL
  HMENTORED
      L

I am told that teens attend church youth groups for a variety of reasons, not all of which are volitional. This is generally not the case in a secular university. In college, attendance is voluntary. If you show up week after week to a campus group or church, it is most likely because you really want to be there.

The people I shared life with in my campus group[7] throughout my undergraduate and graduate studies genuinely loved their God. They had questions. They had trials. They made mistakes. But they were not Christian poseurs. I have rarely seen people sit on a fence for long in a secular university. Some choose a side. Others allow their peers or their past to choose for them.

My freshman year, a campus group director mentored me in methods of studying the Bible—joy unspeakable. Beyond just reading, I could now study *the voice!* The semesters passed quickly, marked by daily phone calls to Dad and Mom. Month by month, my parents were astounded to witness that instead of flickering in a secular environment, my love for God was growing steadily into a strong, sure fire. Two painful conflicts yet awaited us as a family.

"You'll have to put me six feet under before I let you go on that trip," Mom cried. In the spring of 1985, I asked for permission to spend part of the coming summer in Hong Kong. Apart from that Jeep I wanted for my first car, my parents had never said no to a request before. Mom was afraid. Dad was frustrated. Eventually they let me go in a desperate hope that the experience would be disillusioning. They were not surprised two years later when I announced my plans to postpone law school indefinitely and return to Asia. This time, however, Dad would not be silent: "The high school drop-out sweats so his kid can stay in school. The high school graduate sweats so his kid can go to college. The college graduate sweats so his kid can do anything, and you want to become . . . a minister?!"

My parents feared that I was tossing a bright future aside to volunteer half a world away. In September 1988, they waited anxiously for my plane to return from Singapore. Dad wrapped his arms around me while Mom took pictures of the reunion. Holding me tightly, he said, "You're skinny," with a laugh. As he and Mom looked into my dancing eyes, he then added, "And you're happy." I had found what I wanted to live and die doing. My parents never again questioned or doubted that pursuit.

Mom said it was actually embarrassing how much Dad bragged about his minister daughter. Dad's golfing and drinking buddies were playfully grateful when the birth of my son gave Dad a new set of stories to tell. Few feelings match knowing that your parents are proud of you.

A couple years before Dad died, we were talking late at night after watching Jay Leno's monologue. Normally private about his own thoughts, Dad was relaying the sad stories of several of his friends' children. This one on his third divorce. That one with a drinking problem. These on drugs. Then he paused, stared at me, and in a voice cracking with emotion said, "Daughter, I know the reason you turned out different is because of Jesus."

Yes, Dad. But it is also because of you. The love you and Mom have always shown me put a face on God.

```
      A
      D
   I MEX I CO
 THE SC  V MH
 K F STAR M I
 X AND N  AN
     Y GOL DW
   UPE THE H S
     L GLUE
```

Mom grew up in a devout Catholic family on the border of Mexico. A Hispanic beauty with a sixteen-inch waist, Mom met Dad while he was stationed at the local military base. Dad was a six-foot-three skinny high-roller with a greased-back mafia hairdo. Though dazzled by his dancing, Mom fell in love with his mind. She knew she wanted to marry him and become the mother of his baby, which was easier said than done in the 1960s.

Mom was a Mexican Catholic. Dad was an Atheist from the Deep South. Members of Mom's family actually bet on how long the marriage would last. In their pre-wedding counseling sessions, the priest tried to talk with Dad about faith but quickly recognized that Dad was not there to offer himself as a candidate for conversion. Religion was dead for Dad.

Toward the end of her life, my grandmother told me that Dad had a spiritual experience at a Methodist revival when he was around eight years old. "He started walking to church each day carrying his Bible," she said. Then something happened. Dad never shared the details with me, but he was done. He left his well-read Bible on Grandma's table and never looked back.[8]

Nonetheless, Dad promised the priest that he would encourage and protect Mom's faith and the faith of their children. And Mom knew that even though he was not remotely religious, this man she was marrying had a heart of gold.

Dad was definitely the star of our little family, but Mom without question was the glue. Mom was, and still is, the most naturally generous and sacrificial soul I have ever known. She was my angel and she was Dad's anchor. She believed in him, supported him, and was always there to help pick up the pieces when his latest pursuit fell apart.

A **ATHEISM**
X R J N O Y
S K L F I Z S
THE P K R T A
A C **WORD** E W
O R H B E L I E F M
G V D E N Y

Singapore was followed by Australia, and Australia was followed by a wedding. Perhaps through a blog or another book I will someday share the rest of the story. Until then, here are the Cliff's Notes: (A) Our romance began over an intense Ping-Pong match, which (I am annoyed to report) Barry won. (B) Our home and hearts have been filled through the miracle of adoption with three extraordinary children, all of whom are outrageously creative. (C) Our journey was rerouted from the intended path of teaching English in China to serving international students, speaking, and writing books from Missouri.

Over the years, many have asked what it was like to be an Atheist. However, the first question that needs to be addressed is, "What is Atheism?" Merriam-Webster Online offers the following modern definitions of Theism and Atheism:

the·ism \thē- i-zəm\ *noun* : belief in the existence of a god or gods
athe·ism \ā-thē- i-zəm\ *noun* : a disbelief in the existence of deity; the doctrine that there is no deity

Debate continues over whether or not Atheism is actually a belief system and whether or not Atheism should be capitalized. I vote yes and yes, though I recognize that the word *system* will cause some to break out in hives. *System* sounds rather confining in our day, like a tie that is on too tightly. For my part, *belief system* merely means *spiritual philosophies and practices.* I suppose I could shorten that to something like *spp,* but that too feels awkward.

Citing the *Oxford American Dictionary,* Wikipedia defines Atheist as "one who denies the existence of God." More broadly, the word can mean "one who lives without belief in god(s)," which is, arguably, a different concept. Personally, I began as the latter and morphed into the former. Like many other Atheists, in the beginning I was not anti-belief or anti-Theist. I just came to a place where it seemed an unreasonable and unnecessary waste of energy to believe in a supreme being.

Atheists seem to range in reactions from mildly amused to supremely aggravated that their philosophy is defined in the negative. I find the complaint reasonable. Who would want their belief system summed up as a *denial* of some other belief system?

Nevertheless, Atheists are in the minority and definitions are usually in majority hands. Returning to an easily accessible secular source, Wikipedia[9] reports that 2.35 percent of the planet ascribe to Atheism and 11.92 percent consider themselves non-religious. The remaining 85.73 percent either describe themselves as Christian, Muslim, Hindu, or Jewish, or they associate themselves with one of the more difficult to categorize nature/spirit religions (that do not necessarily look to a deity for salvation) like Buddhism, Jainism, and Taoism.

(Note: For a very brief working description of these complex faiths and other spiritual traditions, please reference the Appendix, which contains excerpts from Wikipedia's online encyclopedia. The fact that Wikipedia is a common—as opposed to elusive or strictly academic—source written and edited by the masses is exactly why I chose to reference it for this discussion.

Much has been written exploring valid questions such as whether Hinduism is polytheistic or monotheistic, and whether Buddhism is a religion or a philosophy. These complex issues are well outside of the scope of this book. For my purposes, I will be grouping Buddhism, Hinduism, and spiritualism under the broad category of "Theism" not because they are expressly monotheistic or polytheistic but because in practice they do hold in common a belief in spirit, spirits, and distinct spiritual forces, which seems to directly contrast with the traditional Atheistic belief that there is nothing spiritual "out there.")

A religious source, World Christian Encyclopedia,[10] registered similar percentages: 2.5 percent as Atheists and 12.7 percent as non-religious. On the ground, though, numbers are always muddier. In Asia, political Atheists may pray to and prepare offerings for their deceased ancestors. In the West, practicing pluralists may describe themselves as non-religious because they do not adhere to any one particular belief system.

Often Atheism is used as an antonym for a specific belief system like Christianity or Islam, but semantically the word contrasts with Theism. Though some consider themselves undecided or personally disinterested in the entire discussion, the vast majority of humans on the planet are either Theistic or Atheistic.

We have no way of knowing who the first person was to doubt that their family's god(s) or spirits were real. But historians seem to agree that as a belief system, Theism has the seniority. Atheism[11]—whether defined specifically as "to deny the existence of God" or more broadly as "to live without belief in god(s)"—is the newcomer.

OUTLIVING SANTA CLAUS

Dad began chasing his "first million" right out of high school. He was still in hot pursuit of those elusive dollars when I was born. Dad's mental pockets were stuffed to overflowing with incredible ideas, so our family became quite proficient at packing and relocating. By the time I was fifteen we had lived in five states, nine cities, and eleven homes.

Everywhere we replanted, Mom would unpack quickly, place the boxes in storage, and begin her search for a good local parish. As soon as possible, she would join her newfound church and Dad would wholeheartedly encourage me to attend mass with her.

Without fail, Dad kept his promise to respect Mom's religious commitments, and throughout my childhood he intentionally abstained from discussing his personal belief that faith (of any stripe) was an opiate. Dad believed that spiritual instruction had value and that it was important to protect a child's belief in cultural and religious symbols—like Santa Claus and God—for as long as possible.

So Dad encouraged me to become a person of faith and Mom did her best to expose me to her church's teachings, but religion always seemed hollow to me. Although I appreciated the artistic beauty of the stained-glass windows, and though there was something strangely comforting about communion, it all still felt like some set in a B-grade Western movie. As though a great deal of time and effort went into painting the front of the buildings but nothingness awaited you if you walked through the door—just dust and the mundane sameness of exposed beams and boards.

For me, religious exercise was a waste of time: a stale, predictable, fruitless play. Politely but firmly I informed my parents that I would no longer continue to show up as an actor week after week. "Besides," I added, "I don't think there's really a god anyway."

Dad said that I was only nine years old. Mom thinks I was ten. Either way, they both were deeply saddened for me as their daughter: God had barely outlived Santa Claus.

THINGS NOT TO SAY TO AN ATHEIST

Hyper-simplicity is a malady that affects most of us in one way or another. I add the modifier *hyper* because simplicity alone can be a thing of beauty and wisdom. Hyper-simplicity, however, disrespects the complexity of human thought. No, I am not mocking the truly simple. I am asking—correction, I am begging—that we refrain from reacting to one another's beliefs with poorly thought-out quips and dismissive statements. People have reasons for their beliefs. They may not have evaluated those reasons for decades, but somewhere, somehow belief in something grew to the point of being recognizable and expressible.

Over the decades, I have heard a handful of one-liners about Atheism. I have no desire to shame those who have used these statements, but I would like to suggest that if we are ever tempted to utter one of these phrases in the presence of an Atheist, we pause, seal our lips, tilt our heads slightly, and nod from time to time. The Atheist before us may think that we are just contempla-tive. Seriously, silence is a much kinder choice than the comments I list below:

"All Atheists hate their fathers." *All* is a risky word to select as an opener for most sentences. In this case, however, *all* would probably offend even the most tolerant of listeners. Suggesting that Atheism is always the byproduct of a marred father-image or painful parent–child relationship is simply untrue, as my story alone demonstrates. People become Atheists for many different reasons. Some inherit the belief from their families or cultures. Some default to the belief in the absence of any other discernable, viable option. Some choose Atheism for scientific or philosophical reasons. Some turn to Atheism to mentally survive the realities of an insanely unjust global human condition. Besides, if all Atheists hate their fathers, the inverse truism should be that all Theists love their fathers. Do they?

"There's no such thing as an Atheist." Whenever I ask someone what they mean by this statement, I normally hear a response like this: "Atheism is a belief just like Christianity is a belief. By claim-ing to be Atheists, they nullify their very belief that there is no belief." This often takes me back to a clip from *The Princess Bride*: "You have a dizzying intellect to be sure." Of course there is such a thing as an Atheist. Atheists do not deny the existence of *belief*; they deny the existence of *God*. The two are not the same. God *was* before belief took her first breath. And God *would be* even if belief never breathed again.

"If there's no such thing as God, why do you have to deny his existence?" The premise underlying this statement is that *denial of existence is proof of existence* because there would be nothing to deny if it did not exist in the first place. So . . . since I deny the existence of little green men on Mars to my kids, does that mean they must really exist? Since the scientific community on the whole denies the existence of a tooth fairy, does that mean she really exists?[12]

We can often avoid muddying the waters of conversation unnecessarily by identifying and evaluating the premises supporting our arguments. Both we and our hearers would benefit from such a practice. Though it requires a bit more mental effort, the fruit of that effort is—at the very least—respect, which perhaps is a more powerful force than words.

9

I ADB
H**MEMORIES**
HIXTLCUG
QPT EF YN
L JSWORMS
ZFACTORL
OHK

The sun still rose the day after my decision. Transitioning from uncertainty to Atheism took place peacefully, in part because I did not view Atheism as a seasonal experiment. The non-existence of a god(s) was now a given. As far as I was concerned, the divine was no longer a factor in my life's equation.

Several memories stand out from the next few years. Dad's business ventures kept him busy with frequent travel. When home, Mom and I treated him like the morning sun. Looking back, my respect for Mom only grows. She could easily (and justifiably) have been angry and infected me with resentment toward Dad. Instead, she carefully protected my opinion of Dad when he was gone and consistently guarded my time with Dad when he was home.

The special events I remember through my parents' retelling and photos: the vacation at the beach, Disney, the Peace Gardens, the elaborate birthday parties, Dad teaching my Girl Scout troop.

1

My personal memories though are of the recurring experiences, the ones I could count on. I remember innumerable games of Ping-Pong with Dad—how he would let me struggle to return his serves, how he would cheer my good shots, and how he never threw a game. I remember road trips with Mom through Amish country for the day or to Del Rio every summer—how without fail we would become lost at least once, how she would ask me which way I thought we should go, how she would then wisely choose the opposite direction because I was so dependably wrong. I remember cleaning golf clubs with Dad on Sundays—how we would carefully brush away the dirt and grass, how he taught me to wipe and condition the grips, how all the while we watched Jack Nicklaus, the Golden Bear, make history.

Growing up, I preferred books over Barbies and boxes over whatever came in them. After a move, I would piece the moving boxes together to make elaborate tunnel-homes and painfully retest my ever-failing hypothesis that a three-foot stack of packing papers was as soft as a three-foot pile of leaves.

We had several dogs, all named after Dad's favorite beverages. Martini was a long-haired dachshund who reportedly saved my life twice. Brandy was an Old English sheepdog who had one blue eye and two bad hips. Tequila was a pound puppy who, unfortunately, suffered an untimely death . . . from worms.

Really, it was a charmed life, but only at home. School was a different story.

CB I W
NK**WHAT**TSUHCE
DALUXURYZ
LM**A**SFL
K**RELIEF**
DOORWAYNM
HG I

Personally, Atheism was somewhat of a balm for my fiercely realistic soul. Choosing to believe that there is no God actually resolves a host of spiritually problematic issues. It releases weight from the mind like a hot air balloon dropping sandbags or a ship in a storm dumping cargo overboard. In some ways Atheism makes one feel more buoyant, even liberated, at least temporarily.

If there is no God, then we do not have to question him, her, or them about why the innocent are condemned and the guilty freed—it is simply human error. If there is no God, then we do not have to struggle with why the young mother of three dies and the old molester of hundreds lives to see and abuse his grandchildren— it is simply human sickness striking the weak in different forms. If there is no God, then we do not have to be dismayed that God saw but did nothing tangible to stop genocide—it is simply human greed manifesting itself in unspeakable oppression.

This is not to say that Atheists take the easy way out. I have never met a slacker Atheist, though I have met some who—for whatever reason—did not seem to flex their mental muscles much past the point of "there is no God." The honest Atheist inherits a host of troubling questions and issues with only ever-elusive, universally-disagreed-upon concepts like *greater good, collective consciousness, equality,* and *group morality* as their guide.

The human condition is still overwhelming, but the world-views of Atheists can free them from the additional—and often crushing—weight of spiritual disillusionment. If there is no God, then we do not have to suffer mental paralysis contemplating God's actions or non-actions. We are absolved of Theistic spiritual disappointment.

However, my personal experience no longer affords me this luxury. Without a doubt, I now believe that God *is.* That knowledge leaves me in the uncomfortable position of having to experience spiritual disappointment, of having to struggle with how God could permit the innocent to be falsely accused and the helpless to be shamelessly abused.

In many ways it would be a relief to once again chalk these atrocities up to the human condition alone; to return to a world-view that would deliver me from wondering where God was and what prayer does. But for me, and other sincere people of faith, the tension remains.

Over the years, though, I have experienced a glorious discovery: There is treasure in the tension. The struggle is a doorway. Sincerity in the quest ushers us mysteriously across the threshold, and on the other side is—not answers—but knowing. On the other side is intimacy.

10

People have called upon a handful of adjectives to describe me, but "cool" has never been on that list, at least until very recently, and that, frankly, was a direct result of finding a fabulous pair of embroidered jeans. Creative, analytical, artistic, but never *cool*.

Every class has at least one kid who does not fit in, who is the last one picked when dividing into teams, whom no one wants to dance with, who provides fodder for lunchtime table talk and countless opportunities to hone harassment skills for bullies on buses. I was that kid.

Each August, because of my family's frequent moves, I was the "new girl" somewhere. When it came to team sports, I was woefully un-athletic. When it came to trends, I preferred classical music to the day's boy bands. When it came to leisure time, I enjoyed being with my parents more than going to the mall. Add braces (clear was not an option in the '70s) and acne (in abundance) and you have all the essential ingredients for a preteen's social nightmare.

Up through junior high, only two girl friends' names stand out (Susie and Charlene), and there were no boyfriends to remember. The first crush I recall was in fifth grade. His name was John Borwitz. I fell in love with his ears and the brain between them. "Daddy and Mommy, don't be alarmed when you see him," I cautioned as we approached the school. "I like him because he's really, really smart, but his ears are just like Spock's." *Star Trek* strikes again. Though my parents barely contained their amusement, they were grateful that my values were shifting. The first crush they remember was in kindergarten. His name was Ronnie Russo or, as I called him, "The Muscle Man."

Throughout my tenure as a student—grade school through graduate studies—teachers' opinions have seemed mixed; some found me delightful and engaging, others considered me disagreeable and taxing. In fairness, I could occasionally be a difficult student. Dad taught me (1) respect is earned not automated, (2) do not question your opinion simply because someone else holds a different one, (3) treat everyone, younger or older, as a peer, and (4) do not personalize questioning or being questioned.

Yes, pity the teacher who thought deference came with the bigger desk. I lacked coolness, but I had inherited confidence.

42

GOM
RESPONS
NWACHMO
U **IBILITY**
X I E F S   D A K
O J I N T E G R I T Y
E S T R O N G

As in any belief system, not all who claim to be Atheists are genuine. Some pretenders don the cloak of Atheism to feed their addiction to argument.

The sincere Atheist, however, has been given a gift that, for their sake and for the sake of a needy world, I hope in earnest is used well. Whether attributed to some function or fluke of evolution or to intelligent design, most Atheists have strong minds, and with that strength comes responsibility.

As a young Atheist, I used my strong mind and somewhat skilled tongue to intentionally confuse Theists. I would spin them about on their own words. I would cut them off and reroute them before they made their point. Most grievously, even though I knew that Atheism was historically the newcomer and globally a clear minority, I placed the burden of proof upon the Theist instead of having the integrity to carry it myself. I would look them in the eyes and say, "You believe there's a God? Well then prove it. Prove to me that God exists." Then I would sit back and watch them squirm.

Those we credit for leading us into worldwide philosophical shifts exemplified the tenacity to prove their opinions themselves. As ideological newcomers, they displayed the academic and scientific integrity to bear the burden of proof for their own minority hypotheses.

A familiar example: Well into the seventeenth century, humankind thought the earth was the center of the universe. Nicolaus Copernicus (1473–1543) and Galileo Galilei (1564–1642) did not. They were right. The majority was wrong. Forgive my drama, but Copernicus and Galileo did not therefore each go to the majority and proclaim, "I have an announcement: The sun is the center of our solar system. From henceforth, my minority hypothesis is true until you, the overwhelming majority of humankind, can either prove that the earth *is* the center or that the sun *is not*." These scientists knew that the burden of proof—especially for theories that are in contradiction to what most of the world believes—rests upon the theory's champion, the relative newcomer.

Some may object and state that examples like this are in the realm of science whereas the Atheism–Theism discussion is not. I disagree. Science, philosophy, and religion dance together; their movements influence one another. The suggestion that the earth was not the center of the solar system was considered blasphemous by the religious of Copernicus' day. The philosophical shift that occurred in 1990 when humankind first viewed their planet from the perspective of Voyager 1's lens—when we saw the earth as Carl Sagan's "pale blue dot"—was tangible.

Therefore, I stand my ground: when it comes to confronting and correcting global "givens," I believe that in integrity and out of respect for the beliefs of the majority, the newcomer or dissenting minority should assume the burden of proof. The good news is that humanity can be taught. When confronted with evidence, humankind over time discards traditional beliefs and en masse accepts a new paradigm. Otherwise, *flat earth* would be a society instead of a snack food.

11

WHEN THE RAILINGS GAVE WAY

The social struggles with peers and teachers did not hinder me from running for office, auditioning for plays, or joining the golf team. My parents hoped that trustworthy friendships would be cultivated in these venues, so they encouraged and supported each and every endeavor. Whether by nature or as a survival mechanism, I viewed these extracurricular activities primarily as an opportunity to develop personally, not relationally.

A full calendar, favorable report cards, and even my parents' unfailing love obviously could not buffer me forever. Perhaps due to hormonal changes, the side effects of acne medications, or extended emotional weariness, my resilience to rejection weakened as high school began. The protective railings in my brain that were meant to keep my emotional health centered had been battered for years. When some classmates spray-painted "Zit Britt" on our driveway, the railings finally gave way and I began to descend into a deep sadness. I wept almost daily my entire freshman year.

Dad and Mom experienced an agonizing helplessness as I came home from school each day and spent hours either sleeping or pouring out my heart on the piano. This was the second time they visited a psychologist on my behalf. The first was when they sought advice on how to help their preschooler process being an only child. The Freudian fellow explained that his real professional concern was preparing me for the day I would mourn not being male. The "inevitable" day never came, but some of the stories that resulted from following his advice are hilarious.

Since I refused to see the psychologist, he equipped Dad and Mom with information about depression and a list of warning signs. Knowing what to look for, Mom made sure that there were no sharp objects accessible and that the doors did not lock. Apart from school, she did not let me out of her sight for over a year.

Her concerns were valid. I was considering suicide.

ASKING
FOR
EVIDENCE

Today, around 150,000 people will die. Today, two and a half times that number will be born.[13] Today, 85 percent of the billions in between birth and death will live and work, love and hate, laugh and cry, and invest some measure of faith, belief, trust, or thought in God, gods, or spirits. Does that majority status automatically crown Theism in its many manifestations as Truth? No, but neither is it reasonable to request such a global-given to prove itself every time its adherents utter, "I believe." The weight of proof—if we are going to make proof the crux of the dialogue—rests upon the shoulders of the non-Theist.

When the tables are turned, however, I think the honest Atheist might say, "But God's non-existence cannot with finality be proven." I agree. Why, then, is it considered ethical to ask the Theist to absolutely prove what the Atheist knows cannot be absolutely disproved? Theists are challenged to do the impossible, and then their failure is entered as evidence that their beliefs are misplaced.

This is not a cry for mercy. It is a cry for integrity in the discussion.

As a former Atheist, I now cringe when I hear someone challenge a Theist to bring forth concrete, irrefutable evidence that God or gods exist. Yes, I remember that the challenge was effective in a debate. But winning a debate lost its appeal long ago. A Muslim man helped me see the futility of winning.

We struck up a conversation in a library foyer my senior year in college. I do not remember how the discussion began but soon we were talking about our respective religions and I shifted into debate gear. After an extended pause following a strategic point that I had made, this man's eyes became moist and, in a strong but wounded voice, he said, "I thought that followers of Jesus were supposed to love people." Then he turned and walked away. I never saw him again.

His eyes still haunt me.

In retrospect, my arguments were reasonable, but what does it matter? My words won the debate and my lack of applied love lost his trust. Following that experience, I began listening more and speaking less in discussions. I began to feel an increased responsibility to the human I was interacting with as well as to the unseen others who shared his or her opinions.

Let us return to the unsuspecting Theist being challenged to produce scientifically verifiable evidence that their respective deity exists. First, they are a human soul. Second, as Theists, they do not stand alone but represent the overwhelming majority of humankind. Out of humility, we must see the billions in their shadow.

Perhaps the real discussion here is not about proof but about probability. Given the evidence, which scenario is more likely: the existence or non-existence of God(s)? For centuries, the scholarly Theist and Atheist alike have claimed that both science and the answer are on their side.

If we can be honest enough to consider the possibility that a supreme being's existence or non-existence cannot be proven with finality scientifically, should we then call the debate a draw? Personally, I would rather not. The scientific arguments for and against the existence of God(s) are stimulating—we should not abandon the debate. But we need additional tools if we are to continue making progress in the discussion.

May I suggest the tool of *life*? Glen Davis states the following:

> Ideas have consequences. By forming friendships and examining one another's lives, we can see how religious hypotheses work out in the laboratory called life.[14]

While we are discovering new planets and exploring the mysteries of the human cell, let the earnest Atheist and Theist offer each other the present of presence. Such a gift would give us the opportunity to learn about each other's belief system and view firsthand its most persuasive evidence—the fruit that it bears.

12

```
    A
    H
  FCPEN  LAS
B SEE N I YOU
G PW  D  KREW
TOMORROWC I
  NAMJ   DZ
ASSIGNMENTDY
  I DADDYT B
```

Like many other children, I had an active imagination and enjoyed writing and illustrating stories. My parents laughed for years remembering the mosquito bites that evolved into tales of hippopotamuses climbing through my window to nibble on my arm . . . and the vivid dreams that I would retell and then expand upon for as long as they would listen. Recently, Mom handed me a stack of my first "books" and said with the same unwavering confidence she has always shown in me, "I *still* think they should be published."

My sophomore year, the pen became my therapist as I began writing to weigh life and consider death. Fulfilling a creative writing assignment for drama, I found myself writing a play about a young woman planning her suicide. I entitled the play, *See You Tomorrow, Daddy*. Like the young girl in the story, I was making a list of whom to leave my possessions to, drafting a letter to absolve my parents of responsibility, and preparing for the day.

As an Atheist, the road to suicide was less fraught with moral or philosophical obstacles than perhaps it would be for a Theist of whatever persuasion. There was no god. There was no after-life. Death ended all pain. Why wait for the release when I could initiate it?

But I struggled when it came time to write the end of the play. Capturing in words the finality of saying good-night to her parents and watching the door close slowly for the last time was personally paralyzing. As I wrote, I had to picture my own parents entering my room in the morning, finding me lifeless on my bed, being entirely overwhelmed by grief. No, I would not put the two people who loved my life more than their own through that pain. With tears, I left the play's ending a mystery. Unbeknownst to my instructor, my abandoned plans were turned in with the assignment.

Suicide faded as a viable option, but in the process a dark-ness had crept quietly into my soul. Mom heard it when I played the piano. Dad saw it in the books and music I began to prefer. This would be the last season my Atheism would enjoy emotional neutrality.

```
        E
  A R D W      O S Y
      C U Q U N   J
  C N E A S T V F A W L
    I X T K   D H O S
      Y F E E L R I
    L H I V M A K
  T C O M P A S S U
            U T
```

The West has reawakened to spirituality. From my limited perspective, it seems that the East never went to sleep. An open sea of options now awaits the awakened spirit. If we dare to look closely, though, the coastline is littered with shipwrecked experiments. Not everything that sounds good in the daylight works in the dark. We need wisdom to navigate our spiritual journeys. We need a reliable compass.

For centuries that compass was a substance called truth. Truth was an entity in and of itself. Truth was no respecter of persons; it did not bow to opinion or bend to whim. Collectively though, we have transferred our decision-making trust from truth to perception. "Is it true?" was replaced by "Is it true for me?" which was replaced by "Is it good for me?" and "Does it feel good to me?"

Personally, I still believe in the existence of truth. I believe that truth is frequently findable, occasionally uncomfortable, and always reliable. Truth is not a chameleon that changes its political colors with each generation in the hope of reelection. It is what it is, like it or not.

Still, the fact is that "Is it true?" has been discarded by many as a potential compass for evaluating beliefs. Ironically, truth now seems too subjective. Along with beauty, we have come to believe that truth is in the eye of the beholder.

Truth's demotion is not shocking. We live in a day where revisionism is an art form and spins a multi-billion-dollar industry. We observe opposing groups tilt the same set of statistics to validate their views. We listen to equally educated analysts draw different conclusions about an identical series of events. We view real life courtroom dramas where witnesses swear to contradictory testimonies and experts expound on incompatible interpretations. Drowning in versions of "truth," we throw up our hands and concede that the "real" truth is unknowable. It cannot be absolutely found. Exhausted, we must regrettably call off the search.

Recently, our family vacation road trip took us to New York City. Spatially disoriented from birth, I must have asked a dozen people for directions to the famous intersection of Times Square. The New Yorkers were exceptionally patient and consistent with their reply: Times Square was "just around the corner."

Thirty minutes later and hopelessly lost, I did not question if Times Square truly existed. Times Square *was*, like it or not. The destination was fixed; it had neither moved nor morphed. A few pounds lighter for the extra exercise, we did eventually stumble upon Times Square. My beaming eldest son took a picture, but not of the Coca-Cola sign. Jonathan took pictures of the fascinating street drainage grates that almost ushered a lonely kitty to certain doom in Disney's *Oliver and Company.*

I digress. My point is this: Though an imperfect analogy, truth—like that intersection—can also be hard to find. Yet even then, truth still *is*; it neither moves nor morphs.

Granted, *difficult* to find is a different matter than *impossible* to find. Unlike that intersection, truth is sometimes un-findable. Some mysteries will never be solved. Some questions will never be answered. However, that does not mean there is no answer.

Unknown and even *unknowable* are not synonyms for *non-existent.*

```
C
RIS    CL
ZEM  N**THE**H
   L  GWBY
K I **HOUSE** P F
   EDLUNCHOD I S
NF  FALOST
CHANGEDM
      K
```

With the play and my plans behind me, the depression began to subside slightly, a relief due in part to having changed schools once again. Normal High School (names have *not* been altered to protect the innocent) was bigger than any school I had previously attended. Lost in the crowds, it was like starting all over again. In addition to drama and golf, I joined the speech team and began participating in competitions in the categories of dramatic interpretation and original oratory.

I even accepted an invitation to have lunch with a boy (gasp): a trombone player who wound up spitting on my carpet. At lunch he asked me to accompany him on the piano at an upcoming competition. We were practicing together at my house when, clearing out his horn, he missed the newspaper. Many have explained that spit is just part of playing a horn. Thank you all. The fact remains that the boy spewed saliva on our rug. There was no lunch number two.

Absorbed in my own world and wounds, I was oblivious to the challenges my parents were facing. This last move had deposited our family in the center of Dad's childhood dreams. He had a home on the seventeenth green, a Lincoln Continental Town Car, and a big shaggy dog. Dad loved that house—it represented success for him professionally and as a parent.

Dad, Mom, and I played countless rounds of golf starting on the eighteenth tee, which was a stone's throw from our front door. Crestwicke was a beautiful course, and I still remember driving around in our bright yellow golf cart, losing ball after ball on Hog Alley on the back nine. In the late afternoon, Dad would sit on the porch with a cigar and some wine while we carefully observed players chip onto the seventeenth and putt. I could see it in his eyes: Dad felt that he had finally made it. The problem was that we could not sustain it. Along with the dream came debt that exceeded our income.

With his vision always on what he thought the future would hold, Dad spent today what he hoped to earn tomorrow. In the midst of a conflict, Dad walked away from his job, and his dream began to dissolve. Our family lost the house, the club, and, most painfully, Dad himself for a season.

39

OW
B I **WRESTLING**
D Q B T R A U
F **THE**W　　J I
MAMMOTHD
C I G T S E N S E
Z K M A N T R A
L D P

Some would say that the Atheist disbelieves too quickly. Perhaps. But then, perhaps some Theists believe too easily. Personally, Atheism was a calculated choice. My years as an Atheist began deliberately and ended abruptly.

A quarter of a century later, Atheism still makes sense to me and I am delighted whenever I meet a practicing Atheist. No doubt my past biases me, but I find Atheists to be thoughtful, intelligent, concerned about the world, and grounded in reality. Several other *isms*, however, are more difficult for me to intellectually appreciate, like the fading remnants of religious pluralism or its more vivacious successor, which is sort of a freestyle spirituality.

Religious pluralists generously affirm that all faiths have value, all faiths hold truth, and all faiths ultimately are saying the same thing through different voices and different images. You know the mantra: many roads up the same mountain . . .

Another influential group is uncompromisingly spiritual and unapologetically uncommitted to any singular belief system. I would try to come up with a label or banner to group them by but my guess is that they would probably prefer to stand under open sky.

Theism, Atheism, pluralism, spirituality . . . The possibilities available to the seeking soul are diverse and numerous. Which returns us to a previous challenge: How can we navigate safely through the sea of options?

Perhaps emotions should be our guide. Then again, perhaps not. Imagine that your dearest friend is waiting to board a cruise ship crossing the Atlantic. The captain surprises the attendant by taking the mic, clearing his throat, and saying the following: "This week I'm going to turn off all instrumentation, close my eyes, and navigate by feelings. Don't be alarmed. I have been sailing for decades and I have a real good sense about this trip." Your friend immediately pulls out her cell phone. "What do you think?" she asks. "Should I get on board?" Would you encourage your friend to take a seat, to entrust her life to some captain's *feelings*?

Again, an imperfect analogy, but my point is that it would be socially irresponsible to encourage a friend to appoint emotions (whomever they happened to belong to) as the sole captain of their life's course. Life is too precious to navigate by emotions alone.

I believe this principle also has application for the navigation of our spiritual journeys. Emotions are powerful and persuasive. But are they qualified enough, are they responsible enough, to appoint as the sole directors and assessors of our own or someone else's belief system?

Personally, I do not think so. "It just feels good" is not sound enough to authenticate our own beliefs. Conversely, "I have a bad sense about this" is not substantial enough to dismiss someone else's beliefs.

Wherever its roots are, and whatever its object may be, belief is an authoritative substance. It is formative. What we truly believe—for better or for worse—molds us and influences others through us. We do not live and die in a bubble. Who and what we are affects the earth and all her inhabitants. Our matter lives and our lives matter. Considering the weightiness of belief, "It just feels good to me" does not seem solid enough to base something as globally influential as *a life* upon.

A concern has been lingering in my soul. Attempting to articulate it feels like wrestling a verbal mammoth. I may need to ask for your patience as I struggle to wrap words around what I see.

I am under no illusion that these simple thoughts could somehow cause us to reinstate truth as the prominent cultural compass for decision-making. But I do want to state clearly that I am deeply alarmed by our current direction, by our shift of trust from truth to perception. If "Does it empower me?" and "Does it feel good to me?" are all we feel obligated to evaluate our beliefs and resulting decisions by, we leave ourselves extremely vulnerable emotionally and socially.

The addict would state that drugs empower her. The pedophile would assert that his habit feels good to him. Are we then to nod politely and declare that their personal philosophies on the use of drugs and children pass the acceptable belief test? No. Reason demands more filters beyond "It feels good, right, and empowering" to determine the legitimacy and healthiness of actions and the beliefs that parent them. If we apply the additional filters to the broken of society, in integrity we must also apply those filters to the beliefs and actions of the seemingly more whole.

Since emotions are too, well, emotional and many consider truth to be too elusive, what filters can we call upon? Though not an exhaustive list, I would like to offer four potential filters as a start:

Is my belief system . . . consistent (at its core)?

Is my belief system . . . livable (and not just quotable)?

Is my belief system . . . sustainable (through life-size pain)?

Is my belief system . . . transferable (to others)?

```
        W
        A
   L E    V O H
 P N S T R E S S
 D H I G   H L E Z
 O I C U DRAWN
   M  T F K  O
 N BUTTER J
 A    E X  I M S
 Y
```

When he resigned, Dad sent out résumés, hopeful that another company would hire him quickly. One by one, from Ohio to California, the possibilities collapsed like a house made of cards.

Failure is a wise teacher but a humbling disciplinarian. Dad looked gutted.

As a teen, I perceived Dad during that season as strangely stoic and distant. He made eye contact less, talked less, and laughed less. As an adult, I now recognize that he was embarrassed. At any age, it is a painful thing to watch a good man succumb to shame.

Mom tried bravely to shield me from the stress burning a hole through her stomach. She was in a nerve-racking position. On one side she had me—still on the edge of depression. On the other, she had Dad—teetering on the edge of despair. In between, she was drowning in unpaid bills and mounting credit card debt.

The things Dad had surrounded Mom with were not as important to her as they were to him. Mom treasured relationships. Where she lived, what she wore, or what she drove was not her focus. She just wanted her husband to be happy and her daughter to be whole.

I probably enjoyed our lifestyle a bit more than Mom, in part because I had no idea how much it cost either monetarily or in terms of stress, but also because by nature I am attracted to all things excellent, beautiful . . . and delicious. One of Dad's favorite stories came from visiting a fine restaurant as a family when I was two years old. Starting with me, the waitress asked in a sugary voice, "And would you like a hamburger, sweetie?" Dad and Mom both testify that I replied, "I'd like lobster with drawn butter, please." Speechless, the waitress turned toward Dad, who said, "Well, you heard her. Give her lobster with drawn butter."

Dad was ambitious, but not for himself alone. He wanted to give me everything he never had. I truly appreciated the things, but like Mom, my treasure was Dad's presence. Mom and I never cared what was on Dad's business card. We just wanted him beside us.

38

P I F L A K E G
CONSISTENT
W O D A C K V
R E **A T** U **I T S** B
R S E D J L
A K W I **CORE**
J T Q U T Y F I M S

During critical election years, political posters, ads, commercials, bumper stickers, blogs, and buttons abound. Throughout the entire campaign, the masses and the media monitor funding, critique promises, dissect policies, and analyze campaign strategies. However, all these issues exit center stage immediately whenever there is any hint of a breach in a candidate's character.

Whether the position is that of county sheriff, state senator, or the nation's president, candidates run for office under a microscope. From their use of finances to their personal fidelity, they are examined, questioned, and tested. The results, favorable or not, are broadcast globally:

Did they lie?
Did they misappropriate funds or favors?
Did they disrespect women? Men? Children?

Did they preach what they did not live?

Did they abuse power?

Did they demonstrate unfaithfulness to their covenants or commitments?

Did they show favoritism for the rich or disregard for the poor?

Certainly some take this inspection too far. But in principle, I find the emphasis on character and integrity to be reasonable. When we elect our nation's leaders, our votes entrust them with authority to govern systems that affect our daily lives. It would be foolish *not* to evaluate their personal integrity and interpersonal consistency. Even those apathetic toward elections would prefer not be represented locally, let alone internationally, by a flake or a fraud.

I call upon this example because it seems equally reasonable to me that the savior or founder of our respective faith should suffer the same scrutiny. This filter of consistency could wisely be applied in several ways to a belief system: Are the sacred documents internally consistent and externally verifiable? Is the belief itself consistent with known history and agreed-upon reality? Here, however, I would like to apply the filter to a belief system's *heart*: its savior, its founder, its primary teacher or guide. A president, prime minister, or premier leads a nation in this life. A spiritual savior or religious founder leads souls through this life and into the next.

Webster defines *consistent* as:

1. agreeing or accordant; compatible; not self-contradictory: *His views and actions are consistent.*

2. constantly adhering to the same principles, course, form, etc.
3. holding firmly together; cohering.

As we seek to assess our beliefs, it strikes me as unwise *not* to examine whether our faith or spiritual philosophy's savior or founder is consistent at their core. As with political officers, so it is with spiritual leaders: few care to invest faith in a flake or a fraud.

Who are the primary saviors, founders, or teachers of our personal faiths or philosophies? Bring out the microscopes and let the research begin:

Did they lie?
Did they misappropriate funds or favors?
Did they disrespect women? Men? Children?
Did they preach what they did not live?
Did they abuse power?
Did they demonstrate unfaithfulness to their covenants or commitments?
Did they show favoritism for the rich or disregard for the poor?

A brain surgeon can perform a successful surgery while having an affair or evading taxes. But unlike a physician, a spiritual leader's morality *is* their most convincing credential. I am not remotely implying that character imperfections void all spiritual contributions. But if a discrepancy exists between their teaching and their living, if we cannot be proud of their choices and emulate their treatment of others, we need to—at the very least—pause and take a sober audit of our spiritual investments.

15

V A TXU SYD
 L **TRADI** MURHE
 RWIK **TION**
  SBHZEGN
 TNTEA ICLA
 LWOODSMY

Every December our small tribe of three would make a pilgrimage to Texas to spend Christmas with Grandma Lyle and New Year's with the Ortiz clan. These are happy memories.

Dad was an only child until his mom (Roberta on paper but Bobby to all who knew her) married Harold Lyle and gave birth to two daughters. Becky was a redheaded beauty, a risk taker, and one of Dad's best friends. Lisa was a brilliant blonde, a teacher who seemed destined to instruct at an Ivy League school, and our greatest fear driving the last few windy miles into the piney woods that surrounded Grandma's house. Lisa raced over that one-lane road in her VW bug "like a bat out of hell," Dad would say, shaking his head.

The ultimate Southern cook, Grandma Lyle used bacon drippings like butter and talked about what was on the menu for dinner while you were still eating lunch. "Meal" seemed too anemic of a word to describe what Grandma conjured up in the kitchen.

Surrounded by the aroma of the last feast, the next feast, and a freshly cut Christmas tree, the days passed restfully as we ate sunup to sundown, drowned ourselves in sweet tea, played cards, enjoyed long naps, watched for copperheads, and occasionally took a ride into town.

The day after Christmas we would pack up and leave for Del Rio to spend time with Mom's family. Grandpa and Grandma's house will forever be etched in my memory. They moved into the home as newlyweds in 1933 and lived there until their deaths in 2002. Mom smiles remembering how her parents would add a room each time one of their children married and moved out. Mom was the middle child, bookended by an older sister and brother (Sylvia and Richard) and younger twins (Victor and Emilio). Everyone tried to make it back home for the holidays. The days were filled with laughter and stories, handmade tortillas, and drives across the border into Ciudad Acuña, Mexico.

As an only child, I loved being surrounded by cousins. I was especially close to the twins' boys because they lived in Del Rio and I saw them in the summers as well. Forgive my generalization, but I have found few exceptions: Mexican families are wonderfully and fiercely protective of their own. Internally, there may be conflicts, but woe to anyone who criticizes from the outside in.

October 30 of 1980, we drove down to Texas as usual, except this time two months too early for Christmas and with our possessions in tow. "We're going to stay with family while Dad looks for a job in the South," Mom offered. Observing her worried glances and Dad's tense shoulders, I should have known that a storm awaited us in Texas.

37

LIVABLE AND NOT JUST QUOTABLE

PART ONE

We can be attracted to a belief because of its sheer beauty. Some embrace more pluralistic beliefs because they appear to unify instead of divide, include instead of marginalize, affirm instead of accuse . . . in a word, they are beautiful. It sounds so egalitarian and affirming to assert that all religions hold truth. It feels so freeing and open-minded to cease obsessing over specifics and simply appreciate our collective spiritual journeys.

Many beliefs are quotable and inspiring. Moving beyond their beauty, however, it would be sensible for us to ask if these seemingly enlightened beliefs are soundly *livable*.

Webster defines *livable* as:

1. suitable for living in; habitable: *It took a lot of work to make the old house livable.*

2. worth living; endurable.
3. that can be lived with.

In other words, can we really inhabit our beliefs from their roots up? Can we live with the underlying premises that our beautiful beliefs rest upon? In order to accept a belief with integrity, we must also accept its foundational premises with enthusiasm. Can we?

As an example, let us consider religious pluralism. Diane Eck of Harvard's Pluralism Project pens the following definition of *pluralism*:

> First, pluralism is not diversity alone, but *the energetic engagement with diversity*. . . . Second, pluralism is not just tolerance, but *the active seeking of understanding across lines of difference*. . . . Third, pluralism is not relativism, but *the encounter of commitments*. . . . Fourth, pluralism is *based on dialogue*. . . . Dialogue does not mean everyone at the "table" will agree with one another. Pluralism involves the commitment to being at the table—with one's commitments.[15]

I have never met Diane, but I like the way she thinks and I really like the way she writes. Her definition of religious pluralism is very attractive. In practice, though, most people's pluralism moves well beyond actively delighting in religious diversity to—intentionally or unintentionally—diluting religious diversity in their well-meaning effort to affirm all beliefs and all believers.

"I believe that all religions hold truth. All faiths have value. Ultimately, we are all saying similar truths, in different ways, on the same journey." I cannot count how many people I have heard say something like this. But I can tell you they were some of the nicest people I have ever had the opportunity to meet. Whether as their primary belief or as an addendum to a more traditional faith, most religious pluralists seek to deliberately honor all individuals and cultures by validating their respective belief systems. And they are genuinely uncomfortable with—or even angered by—the narrow notion that there is only one path that leads to salvation and any souls on other paths are lost.

The CIA currently lists the following world religion statistics on their World Factbook:

Christians 33.32% (of which Roman Catholics 16.99%, Protestants 5.78%, Orthodox 3.53%, Anglicans 1.25%)
Muslims 21.01%
Hindus 13.26%
Buddhists 5.84%
Sikhs 0.35%
Jews 0.23%
Baha'is 0.12%
Other religions 11.78%
Non-religious 11.77%
Atheists 2.32%[16]

If we were to apply this second filter of "livable, not just quotable" to religious pluralism (not as it is theorized but as it is practiced), we would ask: What must we first believe, i.e., what premises are assumed, in order to assert that these religions are basically saying the same thing in different ways?

16

UNFAMILIAR TERRITORY

Moving in with his wife's parents at the age of forty because of a financial crisis was humiliating for Dad. He needed grace, and Grandma and Grandpa could offer him none. Grandpa had worked hard his entire life in the same city. My guess is that they perceived Dad's entrepreneurial spirit as plain and simple irresponsibility. Whatever the cause, the peace was uneasy and soon Dad headed back to east Texas to stay with his mom.

When the hoped-for "only a few weeks" quickly gave way to months, I began to struggle with unfamiliar emotions: confusion, anger, and vulnerability. Dad had traveled my whole life, but this felt very different. At the time it did not occur to me that Dad was suffering the same depression that had haunted me. I just felt hurt and even a little deserted.

Del Rio grew up slowly around the sparkling San Felipe Springs along the (not so sparkling) Rio Grande River. The city has a unique beauty, blending the strength of a fertile desert with the colorful warmth of the Mexican culture.

Grandma Alicia moved to Del Rio as a small child. She remains one of the most beautiful and elegant women I have ever seen. Mom thinks I inherited my artistic soul from her. It was not possible for Grandma to leave a purchased garment as is; she was compelled to alter it, to customize it, to improve it. My cousin Jennifer once noted that Grandma loved her family in the same manner: She pointed out a pound here, a pimple there, this weakness, that flaw all in an earnest effort to improve her children and grandchildren. Occasionally uncomfortable, we all knew that she critiqued us because she loved us. Decades later at her funeral, another cousin, Rick, summed up the opinions of the family when he said, "If Grandma didn't make it to heaven, none of us stands a chance."

Grandpa was a strong man who loved his jalapeños and his beer. When sober, he was a quiet, kind soul who helped anyone in need. When drunk, he was emotional and volatile. Having grown up in a home where my parents never even raised their voices, I was frightened on more than one occasion living with Grandpa; a reality that, following each binge, broke his naturally gentle heart. No one really wants to be an alcoholic.

LIVABLE AND NOT JUST QUOTABLE PART TWO

In between acquiring my bachelor's and my master's degrees, I spent two years living overseas in the Far East and Australia. During that time I had the privilege of learning from Islamic, Buddhist, Hindu, Sikh, and Christian friends. Gracious and excellent souls, they generously opened up their homes and their hearts to me—a culturally clueless twenty-one-year-old who smiled WAY too much. They knew the ever-present smile was genuine though, and I knew their concern for me was genuine as well.

From that experience and other travels abroad and here at home, I am so grateful for friends from other belief systems who allowed me to see their faith in action, practiced in real time, up close, not just from the pages of a book. They are the people I think of when I hear someone suggest that all religions are really just different paths up the same mountain.

After thinking about this for years, I can only come up with two viable premises that would support such a statement. First, world religions really ARE saying the same thing or at least have compatible core beliefs.

Do they?

Perhaps if we lined up the sacred texts and cut and pasted with liberty we might be able to come up with something vague like, "Most religions believe in the existence of the divine." But it would be intellectual folly to then conclude that all religions are ultimately communicating complementary messages.

We say such things because we want to affirm the value of each faith. Well, does the Muslim feel affirmed because the religious pluralist believes that Muslims and Jews basically have faith in the same thing? Does the Jew feel encouraged because the pluralist believes that Judaism and Christianity are different paths up the same mountain? Does the Christian feel blessed because the plural-ist believes that Christianity and Buddhism teach the same truths by using different images? Ask them. Ask the committed Muslim, the devout Jew, the practicing Hindu, the devoted Christian, and the sincere Buddhist if they are all saying the same thing or if, at the very least, their core beliefs are compatible. With the possible exception of the Hindu, my guess is that you will hear great unity in their response of "no!"

I am not referring to practices on the edges of these faiths or to great mysteries inaccessible to the general population. We do not have to be world religion experts to identify a faith's central, nonnegotiable core truisms and defining beliefs: Who/what/if is god? Who/what are we? Can we become god? Does god have one or many manifestations? Does evil and/or sin exist and if so what is the path of forgiveness or salvation? What happens after death?

If these foundational beliefs are fundamentally incompatible, is it reasonable to assert that these religions are ultimately saying the same thing?

Which leaves us with premise two: World religions are *not* saying the same thing, but that is okay because the religious pluralist either (1) understands each world religion better than those who practice it, or (2) is enlightened to the point where they can comprehend a reality ("all roads lead to the same god") that either eludes or offends actual adherents of the great world religions.

Any takers for premise two? If so, you are probably not a religious pluralist. Premise two reeks of cultural arrogance, and one of the attitudes that most pluralists want to absolutely avoid is elitism.

So where does that leave us? Frankly, it leaves us uncomfortable. World religions are incompatible at their core. They can all be wrong but logically they cannot all be equally right.

"Many paths up the same mountain" is quotable. However, if our beliefs sound enlightened on the surface yet are not soundly livable at their roots, the painful possibility exists that they may just be pious poetry. We can hang it on the wall if we so choose, but we stand on it at our own risk.

17

```
    P
    R
C V N U M B R
O G   X S H E L P
U W I T H O U T M
S J   K A N O
I   Y T R E S A L F B E
N U N W I N D B
S   Z A N C H O R
        H
```

Mom missed Dad terribly and was extremely frustrated by the circumstances. She was also worried sick for me. As a daughter, I had never been defiant or disobedient. But without Dad to talk to or even a piano to play, I began searching in the dark for something solid enough to lean on. Mom feared that she was losing me, and establishing rules for me at the age of fifteen proved to be a difficult task.

Reeling without an anchor, I began experimenting with two things I had previously never been interested in: drinking and dating (which obviously was not the wisest combination). Alcohol had been the sedative of choice for generations on both sides of my family. Unlike my parents, though, I did not start drinking to be social or to unwind at the end of the day. Whether with my golfing girl friends or in Mexico, I drank to feel numb, which—for a girl who had never even tasted beer before—did not take much at all.

I even ran away once . . . only for an afternoon. Although a feeble attempt, in light of my previous history, it was a clear cry for help. The first place I ran to was a church down the street. I knew the building would be quiet, empty, and safe. The doors, however, were locked. "Figures," I fumed as I kept running around the block to a friend's house.

Along with Mom's love, my cousins' friendships may have saved my life during that time. Vic, a few months older than me, was steady and levelheaded. David, a few months younger than me, was big-hearted and compassionate. He was my friend at school and my roller-skating buddy on the weekends. The three of us laughed a lot and got into trouble occasionally. But overall, my cousins' influence was definitely stabilizing. Every hour with them meant I was not out with other friends whose tolerance for alcohol was much higher than mine and who made a game of turning off their headlights at night as they sped through intersections.

Mom was grateful to be surrounded by family. Still, she knew that we needed to transition as soon as possible.

35

```
         O
         S
S U S T A I N A B L E
W  T H R O U G H  D
E C L I F E G S I Z E C
  D I U R T P A I N
    H N I     F R J
    T M K P A R T L O
  C R I S I S P O N E
              K
```

SUSTAINABLE THROUGH PAIN — PART ONE

As I begin this chapter, a dear friend named Joe is hooked up to over half a dozen life-supporting tubes. He has not spoken for forty-eight hours. Today the doctors encouraged his wife to call in the family, just in case. No one expected this. The specialists had said, "You can look forward to a long, full life."

Joe is a thinker, a guitarist, a lover of rock 'n' roll, a teacher, a mentor, and an all-around great man who loves to laugh. He is young, which means around my age—whatever that happens to be. While living and serving in Scotland, Joe's aches were diagnosed as cancer, so he returned to the States and two weeks ago went up to St. Louis for a bone marrow transplant. During chemo, Joe contracted pneumonia. Now his wife, his two teen boys, and hundreds of friends around the world are praying and believing for a miracle.

Is your belief system sustainable through times like this? Webster defines *sustain* as:

1. to support, hold, or bear up from below.
2. to bear (a burden, charge, etc.).
3. to undergo, experience, or suffer (injury, loss, etc.); endure without giving way or yielding.
4. to keep (a person, the mind, the spirits, etc.) from giving way, as under trial or affliction.
5. to keep up or keep going, as an action or process.

Take your pick as I repeat the question: Is your belief system sustainable through life-size pain? Does it strengthen you to "endure without giving way" when you are deeply disappointed? Can it "keep" your mind when your world is turned upside down?

If not, why? Could it be that you have studied it and practiced it superficially? Then do not slander the faith; scold yourself. But if, to the best of your ability, you have sincerely held the faith and in a time of trial the faith cannot hold you, then your belief system may not be sustainable.

We often think that belief is sustained by our minds or emotions. However, if we believe in Something and that Something is real, then it should have the power to help sustain belief when our minds and emotions cannot. Does it? Does the Object of your faith participate in the sustaining of your faith?

Many, many years ago, a friend told me a story about an experience he had with his son. Little Joel always loved holding his daddy's hand, but since Joel's hand was so small, he could just grip his dad's pinky. Kyle would smile and secure his thumb and index finger tightly around Joel's wrist. Joel thought he was holding on to his dad but the truth was that his dad was holding on to him.

Once when they were crossing a parking lot hand in hand, a large pickup truck suddenly turned a corner, racing toward them. In fear, Joel let go of his dad's hand. Kyle, his grip still tightly around Joel's wrist, pulled Joel out of the truck's path and into safety.

Little Joel thought Daddy was in *his* grip. It took a time of crisis to realize that he was actually in his dad's grip. That lesson can only be learned if you are holding on to someone who (1) is real, and (2) is also holding on to you.

```
        W
EF     T I MDU
LR PRE  V L E
  AG HICCUP
T I  UZP I   T
NLC    L YRHZ I
  WESLACOA
BOSD  NV I
    R
```

In October 1981, a year after arriving in Del Rio, we loaded up the car and moved seven and a half hours away to a home on the outskirts of Weslaco, Texas. Dad had accepted a job offer and, on the surface, life looked good once again. Underneath, something significant had shifted within me. My Atheism had experienced a mutation: It was no longer benign.

Following my depression and the chaotic year in Del Rio, Dad had emergency triple-bypass surgery in March 1982, just a few months after we settled into Weslaco. Together, these experiences brought both depth and edge to my realism. Life *is* painful. Even the strongest among us are still frail.

I have no recollection of ever being annoyed with religious people prior to my sophomore year. It was a free country. If people wanted to invest their time and energy in an illusion, so be it. But sorrow was no longer theoretical. Through a more personal acquaintance with relational and emotional pain, my Atheism morphed into "anti-theism."[17]

Previously when people referred to their faith, I would politely smile and proceed to ignore them. Now I found Theists' blissful chatter about their particular faith or god close to insulting. How could anyone have the audacity to suggest the existence of a god or gods that "hold all power"? How could such beings exist and not use their power to prevent pain? Obviously there is no god. Seasoned by real life, my Atheism had matured: I was more confident than ever about what I believed.

With the sting of social rejection behind me, and the rest of my junior year ahead of me, I looked forward to attending a new school. The partying, regrettably, continued, but graduation was in sight and I had definite plans for the future. I began researching colleges and looking forward to achieving my professional goals: first law school, then law practice, followed by a run for government office and ultimately being appointed secretary of state. I am entirely serious. That was the master plan.

As I began attending Weslaco High School, everything proceeded according to schedule with the exception of one unforeseen hiccup: enter the Bowheads.

34

SUSTAINABLE
THROUGH
LIFEKSIZE
PAIN
BREATH
PART
TWO

Kyle and Joel's true story is an apt representation of my personal faith experience. Several times over the last few decades, circumstances have shaken my mental grip on faith: infertility, autism, breathtaking pain, death, and other trials that—for my wiring—are too personal and private to put in print. I have yelled, wept, grieved, questioned, accused, and wrestled mentally and emotionally to the point where my aching brain felt the cold wind of insanity, and the flame of faith flickered dangerously in the smothering darkness.

But then, each and every time (I do mean that literally), when I am too exhausted to grip faith myself, I become conscious that Another—the Object of my faith—has always been gripping me. I am reminded by the Faith-Giver that faith was not my creation.

His breath sustains the flame of faith even when my mind cannot and my emotions will not.

Beliefs are celebrated in the light. They are tested in the dark.

What do you believe?
    Does it have legs?
    Can it walk, let alone run?

What do you believe?
    Does it have wings?
    Can you soar on its principles into a more noble humanity?
    If so, is that soaring sustainable?

When I began writing this chapter, Joe was struggling to breathe. His heartbeat was irregular. His blood pressure was low. Now, two weeks later, as I attempt to complete this chapter, my vision blurs. Joe's struggle has ended. His smiling face beams at me from his picture on the funeral program.

Along with dozens of other stunned friends and family members, I have walked with Joe's wife, Jayne, these past ten days. I have heard from her lips and seen with my eyes Another who is keeping the flame of faith burning within her—even when the lights go out. Jayne's faith is sustainable.

Sarah, a dear mutual friend,[18] relayed this to us all at the funeral:

As I was thinking about Joe's messages, there has been one in particular that has come to the front of my mind. It was the two-part series he did on heaven and hell. Most preachers might try to portray hell as one of the scariest places you could think of—complete with fire and screaming. But not Joe. Instead he described an image of a man sitting naked and alone on a stone in the middle of the desert. He described hell not as simply a darker version of earth, but a life without love. In contrast he described heaven as unlimited access to perfect love. . . . The first time he shared this message I can remember him coming into the office after writing most of the sermon at a local coffeehouse. His eyes were red and he said, "Every time I read this passage in Revelation, I begin to cry," and in all my years of listening to Joe teach, it was the only passage that did make him cry. The passage that reads,

> Then I saw a new heaven and a new earth, for the old heaven and the old earth had disappeared. . . . I heard a loud shout from the throne, saying, "Look, God's home is now among his people! He will live with them, and they will be his people. God himself will be with them. He will wipe every tear from their eyes, and there will be no more death or sorrow or crying or pain. All these things are gone forever."[19]

Other treasured friends and former students of Joe's knew that it was time to update Joe's status on Facebook. Richard spent days selecting the words and Christie typed them in with fear and trembling—the ground felt holy. The update simply read: "Joe just received his heavenly harp—it's a Gibson."

Rock on, Joe, rock on.

```
        Z
   K  NA
SYNCOHJE  U
   S  ERPATING
BWITHDQ  RY
OL  MEACHF
WFRIENDSANH
   NSYLLABLERVO
COOKIEL  UG
```

The fashions of many decades have returned under the categories of classic, retro, hippie, or eclectic. Many fashions of the '80s, however, are noticeably absent in that lineup. One of the era's accessories was the bow. Small word. Big faux pas.

Somewhere, somehow, someone began starching extremely wide fabric bows, stapling them to young girls' scalps, and calling it fashion. Please do not picture the cute little bows that concerned parents paste on their bald baby girls. Picture B-I-G, bright, bouncing B-O-W-S.

New to school, I was minding my own business, eating lunch in the cafeteria when two bow-headed young women came bopping up to greet me. They stood before me with shiny eyes and starched clothes and introduced themselves while their bows bounced from side to side, syncopating with each syllable like giant metronomes.

All I could do was stare at them in disbelief, so Shawn and Christi continued with their welcome wagon. In unison—it was choreographed—they proceeded to make a grand announcement: "We're Christians!"

Mustering up all the diplomacy I could manage, I replied in a low, firm voice, "Were you two hoping for a cookie? Are you waiting around for some kind of award? Keep your faith to yourself."

And so began friendships that—with the exception of a few benevolent hiatuses—continue to this day.

Shawny was a beauty queen, an honor student, and one of the cherished daughters of a well-respected family. Christi, a pastor's daughter, was also a gifted and intelligent beauty. The two were inseparable, and together they voted to ignore all my warnings. Shawny and Christi were going to be my friends whether I liked it or not.

```
                    D
                    M
        TRANS HNGE
        BQFERABLE
    MRU  PD I COX
A Y N TO L V OTHERS M
  WKCONVEYG  I
      E  HZ PART FK
  LN I DEAQONE
```

If the example of our faith's founder, savior, or teacher is worthy of imitation, if we can agree to the underlying premises that our beliefs rest upon, if our spiritual philosophy has proven sustainable through life-size pain, there is one more filter that I suggest we apply toward a reasonable evaluation of our faith.

Our faith is viable for us. Good. Is it also transferable to others? Webster defines *transfer* as:

1. to convey or remove from one place, person, etc., to another: *He transferred the package from one hand to the other.*
2. to cause to pass from one person to another, as thought, qualities, or power; transmit.

Can our faith or philosophy be passed on and make a meaningful difference in the lives of others, especially others who are not like us?

A dear friend was listening to a conversation among a group of well-tanned, well-off women. They were discussing their spiritual philosophies while drinking designer coffee in the sun. One woman expressed the beliefs of several as she explained, "We just need to concentrate on what we really want in life and then draw the good in the universe to ourselves." My friend was so angry she dared not speak. Later she fumed, "Oh, really?! What about the women in Sudan who are just hoping that they don't get raped today? Are they just not thinking enough positive thoughts?!"

Well said.

I do not believe that it is enough for a faith or philosophy to inspire and enlighten *us*.

I do not believe that it is enough even for a faith to *motivate us* to serve the needy.

I believe that our faith, belief, or philosophy must be able to make a difference not just indirectly through us and our generosity but directly to others, especially the broken in body, mind, or spirit.

Some will disagree with me. That is okay. If you feel that it is enough for a belief to work for you and yours, then be released from the fourth filter. Personally, part of the validation of my faith is whether or not it is transferable across cultural, political, economic, and social lines: Does it have the power to do for others what it has done for me?

Objectors might say, "It doesn't have to. It's enough for a philosophy to empower us to be more compassionate human beings who use our resources to help others, and for everyone else to find whatever path works for them." That argument, however, returns us to the previous discussion on pluralism.

For most Theists, faith is more than a good idea to try on for size, sometimes outgrow, and occasionally trade in. Faith is eternal. Theists do not think of their faith as regional anomalies but rather as universal realities. As a monotheist, my faith is bound to a God who loves each soul on the planet. Therefore, it makes sense to me that my faith—if valid—should have something of substance to say and something of power to give someone besides me.

IN L T A F
THEIR Y O D
U L A H C **WA** K
B O M K E **N** Z P
C R U T C H J S A
I L F **WORDS** J O
C Y N I C I S M T

Along with my brilliant English teacher who was a devout Hindu, Shawny and Christi absorbed the majority of my cynicism, criticism, and challenges over the next two years. They had never interacted so intensely with an argumentative Atheist before, but they were confident that I needed their friendship.

I thought it would be meaningful for you to hear the Bowheads' perceptions of our relationship firsthand. *Viva* Facebook! Decades after our friendship drew its first breath, Christi and Shawn were happy to send the following quotes and memories to add to this story:

> *Christi:* I never thought of Alicia as angry; I saw hurt. I also saw someone who was so intelligent that blind faith was an unfathomable concept. I always felt we all loved each other even though we disagreed! I believe so strongly that if people would discuss with love and GREAT HUMILITY, more would work out. That is one of Shawn's great gifts: softness of spirit and humility.[20]

Shawn: Alicia and I were in almost all the same classes our senior year. I remember one time in our English class, we were asked to write a paper. I don't remember what the assignment was exactly. I certainly don't remember what topic I chose. However, I do remember very clearly what Alicia wrote her paper on: "How Christians use Christianity as a Crutch." The day we were turning our papers in, Alicia shoved her paper at me and said, "Read it!" I did and was devastated. She just laughed. It hurt me. But as strange as it sounds, we still remained friends. . . . We were drawn to each other. [21]

My tolerance for hypocrites, frauds, and poseurs was unmercifully low. People did not have to be geniuses to earn my respect, but they did have to be genuine. Shawny and Christi's sincerity was indisputable. Confrontation after confrontation, Shawny would respond, "I don't know the answer, Alicia. But I do know that God is real!"

The Bowheads' friendship was precious to me not because they possessed answers but because they possessed humility. Their acknowledged ignorance, i.e., "I don't know," enhanced—not eroded—their credibility.

Shawn: Because Alicia questioned my beliefs, it forced me to search the Scriptures. I always knew in my heart what I believed, but proving it to someone else was a very different thing. Alicia analyzed everything. It had to not only make sense to her—she had to see proof, to experience it. She wasn't about to accept something just because someone told her to. She just was not a "follower." [22]

Shawny was correct. By nature and by nurture, following was not my forte and I was equally disinterested in being followed. I just wanted to learn and think independently, critically, and without censorship.

32

H   O
C **TRANS** J I K A
W B **FERABLE**
TO X **OTHERS** G
V R D R A F T E D N
A F H E L L B G L I
E Q U C **PART** X S Y
Z F R E E M D **TWO**
L

I cannot think of any greater hell on earth than that being lived by those in sexual slavery. The statistics are paralyzing. Each year, almost a million humans will be trafficked across borders to be enslaved in the sex trade. Most are women and children. Many were sold by their parents. All will live their lives being raped by monster after monster. Their days are marked by endless pain and abuse. Their bodies are ravaged by disease. Their children grow up witnessing and eventually being drafted into the horror.

What would our faith or philosophy say to them? Perhaps, "Concentrate on what you want and draw the good of the universe to yourself." Or, "Find a happy place." How about, "The terror you are experiencing is because you are paying for sins in a past life. Endure the suffering in the hope of attaining a better life in your next reincarnation."

Is our faith *transferable*? Do our beliefs have the power to free and bring hope to the helpless?

The speaker's voice cracked with emotion. Dr. Beth Grant works with women who have been sold to the brothels of Bombay. As young as eight years old, a hundred thousand women work behind bars while children play under their beds. With her co-workers, Beth has established Homes of Hope for those trapped in forced prostitution. She spoke of children receiving education and safe shelter, of women escaping slavery and working with dignity, of weddings and funerals, and, most of all, of the radiance that is reflected on women's faces as they encounter the One who died to set them free:

> What a difference Jesus makes. For you and I? Yes. But for millions of women and children around the world who are literally in hell, the promises of God are just as real and relevant. The promises that are good for a woman here in the boardroom in Baton Rouge are just as good for those women that are in the brothels of Bombay. There is no difference. His promises are real. They are powerful. For those who turn their face toward him, he brings change and new life.[23]

That is transferability.

Sadly, transferability—the lack thereof—was one of my greatest charges against Christianity as an Atheist. Simply put, I was wrong. I should have researched my accusations and taken the time to learn if followers of Jesus were touching the "untouchables" of the world. I should have contrasted the different results between purely secular rehabs for drug addicts and faith-based centers like Teen Challenge. I should have contrasted the results of spiritually neutral efforts to serve women and children imprisoned in the sex trade to unapologetically Jesus-centric efforts like Grant's Project Rescue.

Since I accused others freely as an Atheist, I feel compelled to apply this filter fully to my faith as a Theist: Do my beliefs hold their power when transferred to others?

```
      N
      K       D
  ARPON  MINA
SCFWELLHC
PIDO  UTV  T
YBALANCEDAEQS
VOC    ZYPES
DFAVORITET
TRILA    FKE
```

In addition to arguments, our two years together were filled with fun. Whenever Shawny and I had a class together, without fail she was the teacher's favorite and I was not. Shawn remembers a class project on owning property where I did all the research, wrote the paper, made the presentation, and then she came up at the end with a cake, cut it into pieces, and gave everyone a sample of "real estate." "Our chunky teacher gave me a higher grade," she recounted recently, "and you were furious." Indeed.

On another occasion, Shawny had her eye on a new boy sitting in the school office. Stepping in as her spy, I walked through the door, took a seat, and, like any good girl friend would do, began collecting information.

"So," I queried, "where are you from?"

"The juvenile detention center," said the boy with big brown eyes.

"Oh," I replied, trying hard to act like I expected such an answer. "What were you there for?"

"Stabbing a lady."

"Hmm," I offered in a pitch too high. I was beginning to think this was *not* a good match. "Why did you stab her?"

"I didn't like the way she walked."

"We-e-e-e-ll, thanks for talking."

Shawny still laughs remembering how I opened the door and walked out of that office as straight as a pin.

So many stories . . . in all, the fiery debates were well-balanced by shared laughter. I was drawn to Shawny and Christi. Their faith I dismissed as heartfelt but misplaced: the errant byproduct of idyllic circumstances. One day, real life would no doubt shatter their illusions. But for now, their inner contentment—whatever its source—was soothing. I was glad they called me friend.

My parents were also grateful for the girls' friendship in my life. The fact that they were "too religious" was far outweighed by the fact that they had moral convictions. With my other friends, I dated, danced, and partied in Mexico. The drinking, however, ended abruptly my senior year the night a friend and I were introduced to a new mixed drink. I liked the effects of alcohol, but I never liked its taste and, consequently, felt my drinking was well under control.

Though Dad and Mom did not believe it was in my best interest to give me a list of rules, Dad did, on occasion, offer principles, one of which was: "Drugs are stupid." Halfway through the new drink, I felt fear. This was a taste I could grow addicted to. This could become a drug for me. It was the last drink I ever had.

THE FOUR FILTERS APPLIED TO MY PERSONAL FAITH

I would obviously be a consummate hypocrite if I offered you these filters without first applying them to my own faith. After twenty-five years of testing, I am glad to report that my faith in Jesus is still sound. Filtered through times of unexplainable pain and indescribable joy, this faith endures and actually becomes more precious to me each day.

Filter One: *My faith's savior, Jesus, is consistent to the core.* Without exception, I am proud of the way he lived, and it would be a high honor for anyone to suggest that my life resembled his. He did not lie but spoke the truth even when it was costly. He did not misappropriate funds but chose to live simply. He showed scandalous respect for even culturally untouchable women and men and consistently made room to value children. He lived what he preached and preached what he lived. He demonstrated great humility in the use of his great power. He was faithful to his covenants and commitments. He called the rich to accountability and befriended the poor in body and spirit. Thousands of years following his death, such consistent character still captivates and inspires me. Though its overuse has made it sound trite, I mean these words with all my heart and mind: I want to be like Jesus.

Filter Two: After sincere and continued evaluation, I can state soberly that *my faith—though quotable—is also livable*. I have considered its roots, its underlying premises, and can accept them with intellectual integrity. Although they are at times uncomfortable and controversial, I have yet to identify and examine a foundational premise that I cannot live with.

Filter Three: Life's most agonizing moments have revealed that *my faith in Jesus is sustainable*, even through life-size pain. When intellectually my mind has been too disillusioned and exhausted to tend to the fire, when emotionally my disappointment and anger have depleted all the oxygen in the room, the flame of faith still burns—sustained not by my pampering but by the actions of Another, the Author of my faith.

Filter Four: I have witnessed firsthand in countries around the world that *faith in Jesus is transferable to others*. Jesus' message is meaningful and relevant to people from vastly different backgrounds and experiences than mine. Its transforming power is not restricted to those who share my demographics. The tangible hope that faith in Jesus ignites crosses all—yes, I do mean *all*—political, cultural, and economic boundaries. It works for the broken victim and it even works for the repentant accused. It works in the garbage dumps and it works on Wall Street. It works in the bush and it works in ivory towers. With joy I have seen with my own eyes, and through the lives and stories of trusted friends, that faith in Jesus is relevant, accessible, and effectively transferable to others.

Rest assured, I have no intention of retiring from the evaluation of my belief system. But knowing that it has repeatedly passed through these filters decade after decade makes what I would like to say next all the more meaningful for me.

```
    H   B
 I S R T   W I
  P A E S K O G N
RECYCLABLEMCOR
LEODP  QIT
  CNA VBO  E
  HSOCIETYNA
D I A L O G U E M
```

Shawn and Christi affirm that, in two years of often heated dialogue, I was never at a lack for words. However, I do distinctly remember one of their arguments that left me speechless. Exasperated, one day Shawny retorted, "Well, what about this: A man prayed for a lady at a meeting and she was healed. I know her. I saw it with my own eyes. How do you explain *that*?!"

This was unexpected. I had no immediate response. Surprised by my sudden silence, Shawn went on to talk of other spiritual experiences. My brain hurt. I knew Shawn too well to dismiss her as a lunatic or a liar. She had seen something for sure: I could not explain that reality away. The supernatural stumped me.

Before we all knew it, graduation was upon us. The Bowheads received all sorts of nice people awards, like "most likely to succeed." Our Hindu English teacher, Mrs. Subrahm, gave me the

English Award, mentioned something about the potential of my pen, and handed me an enormous dictionary. ("Decent writer. Lousy speller.")

All four grandparents came into town for my graduation— even Grandpa Britt, whom I saw only a handful of times my entire life. Along with my whole family, Shawny and Christi held their breaths as I walked up the steps to deliver the salutatorian address. My speech was entitled, "A Recyclable Society." An excerpt from my original manuscript (faithfully preserved through the years by my mother) is below:

> If I had to choose one word to describe the society in which we live it would be *recyclable*. Go on, apply for the job. If you don't like it you can always quit. . . . No one is taking responsibility for anything anymore. No one is making things work. Everyone expects things to work for them. Where's that self-confidence? Where's that inner-motivation? Why is it that everyone is living for themselves TODAY and worrying about tomorrow when it comes, if it comes?
>
> It's time for this lack of self-esteem to cease. And we're the ones to do that, because we're the class of 1983 and we have morals, and we have ambition, and we have goals. And there is nothing to stop us from making those goals come true and making those dreams reality.
>
> So let's take responsibility for what we do. Let's make that one marriage last a lifetime. Let's put everything we've got into that career, whether it be as a housewife or a U.S. Senator. . . .
>
> And let's see in ten years at our class reunion if the class of 1983 fulfilled the potential we all know we have.[24] Let's see if we didn't have to recycle our lives. Let's see how many of us didn't have to settle for second best, because we're not second best. The Class of 1983 is second to none!

Shawn's mom whispered incredulously in her ear, "She sounds like a Christian." Equally astonished, Shawn replied, "I know." My parents were beaming. Mom said Dad was so proud she thought he would pop. Speaking would one day become part of my primary profession, but this first time was the one and only time Dad would ever be in the room.

The future looked bright. From Shawny's and Christi's perspective, I was confident, intelligent, deeply loved by my parents, and destined for professional success. They feared I would never feel the need for God.

They were right: As an Atheist, I never did feel the need for God.

However, we all underestimated how much I needed a priceless gift they had already given me.

```
        S
  M I D U    G L A
  S N L W THING R
    C I D Z A K C M
    E   J ONE T
F A P G R O W T H P J I K
  N E R V O U S A B
```

God awakened me to his existence when I firmly believed that I was not sleeping. He offered me his love before I even thought of offering him my life. In the language of relationship, God assumed all the risk. Loving him was easy.

However, in the years following the encounter it has been extremely gratifying to realize that I not only *love* God, I really, really *like* God. There are five things in particular that this former Atheist really likes about God.

One of the primary reasons that the secular university was such a greenhouse of spiritual growth for me is that I was in the grip of a God who delights in sincere questions. This is the first thing that I like about God.

When God arrested me that day in June, it was as though someone pulled up the shades, threw open the windows, and invited morning sunlight and fresh wind into the stuffy attic of my mind.

The famous phrase from John Newton's hymn "Amazing Grace" made sense: "I once was blind, but now I see." And the more I saw, the more questions I had.

What a relief it was for me to discover that this continual questioning did not make God nervous. Interrogatives do not irritate God. Emotionally charged query does not shut God down. Over the past quarter century I have come to the conclusion that God is, after all, rather secure.

The problem is not that we *have* questions. The challenge is what direction our hearts and heads are facing when we *ask* questions. Do we question with a posture that is open or closed to the existence and involvement of God? Do we question with an attitude that is humble or hardened toward receiving insight, instruction, and correction?

Personally, I have found that God takes pleasure in an inquiring mind. God delights in sincere questions. Unfortunately, not all questions are sincere.

Webster lists the following synonyms for *sincere*: honest, pure, true, wholehearted, heartfelt, hearty, and unfeigned. In other words, to be sincere is to be in all respects *genuine*.

Genuineness compels us to resign from excuse-making and take full responsibility for our part. Genuineness calls us to be emotionally honest in the identification of our actual motivations. Genuineness demands that we not strategically position secondary or tertiary issues as though they were primary.

People ask disingenuous questions for a variety of reasons. Some—who relish the rush of debate—value winning (as opposed to growing) as the desired end of argumentation and declare that all means toward that end are morally neutral. Some—to survive or get ahead—have ceased asking themselves honest questions so it is virtually impossible to sincerely question others. And some—directly or indirectly—question God insincerely because by casting doubt on God's character or actions they can justify releasing themselves from adherence to God's values or compliance with God's ways.

What questions do we direct toward God? Are they all *sincere*?

If our questioning is actually a strategic effort to protect our moral, behavioral, and interpersonal status quo (i.e., we like our lives the way they are, thank you, and we are not interested in change), may we at least have the integrity to not hide behind a smokescreen of false accusations against God.

Who on earth appreciates insincere questions? Sincere questions, however, are a delight to God, and I really like that about him.

```
      P  A
  C    DR I W
N THEY'RE KAGYST
  AB   VUSYK
EVERYWHERE
  L I F    N  N
 I WSDOKT   T
HPACKAGELOK
```

For reasons I never understood, Shawny and Christi felt compelled to give me little green Bibles. I used them as bathroom paperweights. They also gave me something else that I had no idea I needed: the present of presence.

Though admittedly a lovely wordplay, I use this phrase in earnest to describe what I have come to believe is one of the most transformational substances we can offer others in our lifetime. By "the present of presence" I mean purposeful proximity, intentional engagement, with-ship.

Shawny and Christi came close enough, long enough, that their God (whom I am now convinced *is*) echoed his reality through their humanity. Unbeknownst to us all, something deep within me was about to awaken.

Consciously, though, as far as I was concerned, my personal

interaction with Theists had only served to strengthen my certainty that there was no god. Intellectually, my commitment to Atheism as a belief system had not wavered. Emotionally, I possessed no nagging questions or doubts. That summer as I prepared to go to college, god or gods were not remotely on my mind.

A few weeks after graduation, I called Susie, a friend from grade school back in Illinois, and asked if she wanted a guest for one or two weeks. She was thrilled, so I packed up my bags in preparation for the trip. A day or so before I was scheduled to fly out, Susie's mom made an unexpected phone call.

"Alicia? It's Mrs. Sokol. We're glad you're coming to visit. I wanted you to know that this summer when you come, you're going to meet Jesus."

Pulling the receiver away from my face, I stared at the phone in disbelief. My first thought was, *They're everywhere. These Christians are everywhere.* My second thought was, *I wonder if she wears a bow too. Maybe it's just part of the god-package thing.*

"Mrs. Sokol," I finally replied, "there's no Jesus to meet."

Hanging up I thought, *Awkward. Well, at least we got that discussion out of the way.*

THING
TWO

AND

THREE

The second thing I really like about God is that walking with God sharpens, not dulls, my mind.

Through the encounter, God definitely had my attention. I was ready to learn. What I did not anticipate, though, was an increase in my *ability* to learn. When God awakened me to his existence, my critical-thinking skills expanded and my creativity exploded. Looking back, that surge makes sense: God was mentoring me.

I am not using this word *mentoring* figuratively. God is not an inspiring picture hanging stationary on a wall that we are to admire, meditate upon, and reference in conversation. God has dimension. God is dynamic. God is present. As I think with God, read God's words, sing to God, remember God throughout the day, I sense God's gentle, engaging instruction.

Most would treasure being mentored by an Einstein, Confucius, Gandhi, Socrates, Mother Teresa, or Beethoven. Walking with God I found myself being mentored by the One who designed their brains.

Reason and experience were no longer forging the path alone. Now they were accompanied by faith. Faith opened doors for my mind and my life that I could have never before imagined. Walking with God has broadened, not narrowed, my base of knowledge and experience, and I really like that about God.

The third thing that I really like about God is that he is not a fool.

As a young Atheist, I remember thinking, *There is no God. But, if by some chance I'm wrong, he, she, or they ought to be reasonable enough to be satisfied with the fact that I'm basically a decent human being. I clearly do more good than harm.*

Sometimes we view spirituality as a divine golf game: We hated getting that double bogey on the last hole, but if we get a couple of birdies in before the end of the round, we can still shoot par. Or we think of spirituality as a moral checking account: Debits are regrettable, but as long as we make more deposits than withdrawals, we can still end up "in the black."

We hope that community volunteerism balances familial vandalism and that charitable giving balances uncharitable living. The problem in this line of thinking, though, is that God is not a fool. He cannot be bribed by any amount of deposits (i.e., good deeds) to turn his face away from our debits (i.e., wrongdoing). Frankly, I would have lost respect for God if the child molester could purchase pardon by donating a million dollars to the church.

Forgiveness, however, is a different issue. An ocean of forgiveness is available to each of us. No matter what we have done, when we come to God sincerely, he forgives us freely.

Forgiveness? Yes. But bribery? No. God is not a fool, and I really like that about him.

24

Arriving in Illinois midsummer of 1983, I was ready as always for a good argument. Honestly, I delighted in debate, especially when the discussion surrounded religion. Mrs. Sokol, however, was disinterested in taking on my mind or my tongue. She aimed straight for my heart.

"My God knows your name, Alicia," she would say perhaps once a day.

What? What is this woman talking about? I thought as I shook my head and continued with whatever I had been doing.

"My God knows all the pain you've experienced," she would add from time to time.

This one stung. No one had the right to assume they knew anything about the pain I had seen and felt over the years. Normally, I would have verbally confused and abused anyone who dared to speak to me like Mrs. Sokol did. But she was just too nice of a person to yell at. So I did the next best thing: I just ignored her.

"Want to come to church with us Sunday?" she asked.

"Are you kidding? Of course not." I laughed.

"Want to come to church with us *this* Sunday?" she asked again, days before I flew back home.

By this time, I knew that this woman would never leave me alone until I went to church with her.

"Fine. Okay. I'll go."

Sunday came and I climbed into the car in my finest purple miniskirt. All I had to do was survive the hour or two without being caught rolling my eyes, without exploding in laughter, and without initiating a debate. How hard could that be?

Walking toward the entrance through the gravel parking lot, I noticed that other churchgoers were staring at me.

Must be the purple, I thought. *Then again, looks like the average age here is approximately 912. Maybe they're trying to remember if they know me or not.*

I was wrong. They were not trying to remember. They were eyeing the young woman they had been praying for all week. On the previous Sunday, Mrs. Sokol had "requested prayer" for "the pagan" staying with her. (Pagan?! I was not remotely a pagan. I was an Atheist, and the two words are not interchangeable.)

The church building was very small and very simple. I sank into the back pew, looked around, and sighed, *I'm already bored. Hopefully this won't take too long.*

That day on June 26, I sat in a little white building expecting *nothing.* I was not there to begin a noble truth search. I was not there to embark on a spiritual pilgrimage.

I was not there to find a god: I was there to get rid of a Christian.

28

```
       L
   T E I      W
   THINGKY  O
   R  DSFOURAS
   CVY  PBEJ  UR
   MOMENTUMZ
   AEDSCOMPLEX
   S      GN
```

Being an Atheist as a young adult is somewhat of a different matter than being an Atheist later in life. Our social, emotional, and intellectual development influences our belief systems. Apart from the encounter that I sincerely believe would have arrested me at any age, I cannot foresee any way in which real life could have done other than cause my Atheism to gain more momentum.

Philosophy, more than science, had led me into Atheism. Personally, I think there is more art in science than is generally acknowledged, and that it is unfair to the sciences (be they the realm of the astronomer or the physician) to require absolute objectivity in their contributions.

Identifying facts can be accomplished somewhat objectively (e.g., "Your temperature is 105."). But interpreting facts is a subjective skill that best serves others when exercised with humility (e.g., "There are many possible causes, so let's run some tests."). The human lens is magnificently contoured by personal experiences, unique abilities, and acquired knowledge. Together, our multifaceted sight enables us to absorb and assist the world more creatively and effectively. In other words, I believe that human subjectivity is more of a blessing than a curse.

Probably because of this perspective, the scientific arguments for the non-existence of God were interesting to me, but I never found them completely convincing. The philosophical arguments for the non-existence of God, however, were quite compelling.

How could a god exist and permit such horrors? How could a god exist and permit such confusion and contradiction in how people viewed and worshiped him or her? As an Atheist, I was not trying to cause trouble; I was just trying to be realistic.

So you can imagine how supremely relieving it was to discover that God is the *ultimate* realist. This is the fourth thing that I really like about God.

Life is not tidy. Pain coexists with joy. Opportunity dances beside injustice. Shameless waste lives within mocking distance of abject poverty. In the waiting room of real life, one celebrates a birth while another mourns a death; one hears the word *benign* while another hears the word *malignant*.

Real life is really complex.

My angst over life's complexities did not vaporize in the heat of the encounter. That life-altering experience was not followed by a peaceful, "Ah, it all makes sense now." It did *not* make sense and now *I was a part* of what did not make sense.

Though some describe the message about Jesus ("the gospel") as *simple*, to my relief God himself can never be described as *simplistic*. God neither dilutes discrepancy nor ignores complexity.

God does not conveniently edit out the uncomfortable. He is the ultimate realist.

Spiritually seeing God's wholeness did not blind me to the world's woundedness. Over the years, my sensitivity to injustice and pain has only heightened. Walking with God, I still see life's complexities—but now that sight is attended by hope and complemented by a renewable strength to fight. Relationship with this realistic God has made me, both in thought and action, more (not less) in touch with the true aches of humanity. I really like that about God.

```
T I        U
A H N  O X L W D
PRESENCE A
U Y P  S E    T S
R E N C O U N T E R D A G
   T N A M E  R
O R G A N X A M S L
            N Y
```

An instrument that sounded like a *really* old organ began to play and, on cue, everyone stood. What happened next will always remain a cherished mystery to me. I will do my best to describe the experience.

The people in the little white building lifted their voices and began to sing. That is when it happened. That is the moment the encounter began.

I was standing with them, but my awareness of everyone and everything else in that room faded instantly. What was left was not nothingness but a Presence: a sure, full, distinct Presence.

Motionless, I was alert but not fearful. It felt like I was surrounded by a sea yet instead of drowning, I was breathing for the first time in my life. The ocean, the Presence, began flowing over me, flowing through me, gently, yet with power.

Still immersed in the Presence, it felt like a waterfall opened above me. These waters—sparkling, fresh, alive—began surging through me. They were forceful and somehow I could see and sense the waters breaking chains off of my mind, dislodging chunks of dirt from the fabric of my soul.

I had no knowledge of anything happening outside of the encounter. The singing, the speaking, the praying . . . I missed it all as the experience continued throughout the entire service.

Love, thick and purposeful, enveloped me. A Presence was calling to me. Without any question or even a hint of confusion, I knew its name as I know my own name.

To the best of my ability, I had studied different world religions because it only seemed fair to give them equal time in debate. Honestly, in the midst of that encounter, I think I would have been open to any name. But I only heard one.

The name did not repeat itself over and over like a broken record. Instead, it sounded within me like a sustained but distinct tremor radiating from my core.

One name: Jesus.

```
K I S     D S
L THING PO
Q T U R M     B L A
S T U   N M FIVE C G
I K N O W A B L E
J E I R   E S
D H O L R I S K
```

The fifth thing I like about God—and this is the thing I like the very most about God—is that he is *knowable*.

Yes, I am aware of the definition:

know \nō\ verb
1. to perceive or understand as a fact or truth; to apprehend clearly and with certainty.
2. to have established or fixed in the mind or memory.
3. to be cognizant or aware of.
4. to be acquainted with as by sight, experience, or report.[25]

More than anything else, this thing about God surprised me. I would not have been shocked if, following the encounter, God had proceeded to download some divine "do this" and "don't do this" list. But I was stunned when what God gave me was *himself*. Not a philosophy to ponder or a task to accomplish, God is a Person to be with and to know. I *know* the living God:

1. I perceive God as fact.
2. God is fixed in my mind and memory.
3. I am aware of God.
4. I am acquainted with God by experience.

To think that we could know everything about God is like thinking we could wrap a tiny walnut shell around an enormous watermelon. Our finite minds obviously cannot fully comprehend the infinite. But since we cannot know *all things*, does that mean the only option left to us is knowing *no thing*? Of course not: Much is known about God, enough for us to spend ten lifetimes living if we had the opportunity. God is knowable and I really like that about him.

Almost all of us have beliefs about God. Even if we do not particularly believe *in* God, most of us have an assortment of beliefs *about* God.

How were those beliefs formed?

We become annoyed when people draw conclusions about who we are when they do not even know us. We become aggravated when people make assumptions about why we do what we do without ever giving us the chance to speak for ourselves. We call that arrogance.

Yet we do the same thing to God on a regular basis. We frequently draw conclusions about who God is without really knowing him. We regularly make assumptions about why God does what he does without ever giving him the chance to speak for himself.

Are we willing to lay aside the conclusions we arrived at on narrow one-way streets, transition to a two-way street, and offer

God the same courtesy we demand that others offer us? Will we risk asking God to speak for himself?

I invite you to reconsider the portraits you have painted of God. I invite you to risk holding that portrait up toward God and comparing your version with the Original. I even invite you to believe. Let me emphasize what believing is *not*:

Believing does not mean that you will no longer have questions.

Believing does not mean that you will turn off your brain.

Believing does not mean that you will enter into a relationship with God in which you can bribe him to do your will.

Believing does not mean that you will live in denial about real, raw life.

Believing does mean that you can *know* the living God.

You *can* know the living God.

26

ENTERING THE MYSTERY

This is God, I thought to myself. *Shawny's God. Christi's God.* My existence was being interrupted by the God of the Bowheads.

From time to time, one or two or twenty people have called me stubborn. (Personally, I prefer the adjectives *clear-minded* and *purposeful.*) Stubborn I may be. But stupid I am not. There is only one reasonable response when a God—whose reality you have denied—pursues you.

When this pursuing Presence caught up with me, it did not crush me with anger or cause me to cower in the corner with shame. Instead, the Presence covered *me*—my failings, giftings, memories of the past, hopes for the future, unspoken thoughts, and even my blasphemies.

In the encounter, love itself was redefined. God's love had a backbone. God's love was strong and volitional: a trust-inducing blend of unreserved devotion, full knowledge, and acceptance so lavish, so complete, that it was healing.

The one reasonable response? Surrender.

God *was.* My worldview was irreparably altered: *What does this mean? What will this mean for my future, my dreams, my family?* I wondered.

Though I had no answers to any of these questions, I did know that it would be intellectual and emotional suicide to deny the reality of what I was experiencing.

It was true that God's existence would change everything. But I had never intentionally lied to myself before, and I was not going to start then. I could not live in denial of the encounter even for the sake of maintaining my life's equilibrium.

Yes, my spirit whispered. *Yes, I believe.*

With that response, my soul was suddenly and surprisingly released. I felt carried. The realization that God *was* and that God wanted me was overwhelming. A warm hope began to fill me.

I had never considered myself a prisoner, but instantly I knew that I was free. I had never considered myself dead, but now I knew that I was alive.

The encounter was depositing within me a gift: faith—a living, growing substance not made by human hands. Escorted by faith, I entered an indescribably beautiful, stunningly satisfying, adventure-filled mystery:

Truth is *not* dead.

God has always lived.

Life is full of pain.

Death is but a door.

And the God who *is*, aches to love us.

APPENDIX: THUS SAYS WIKIPEDIA[26]

Animism, from Latin *anima* (soul, life), commonly refers to the belief systems that attribute souls or spirits to animals, plants, and other entities, in addition to humans. Animism may also attribute souls to natural phenomena, geographic features, everyday objects, and manufactured articles. Religions that emphasize animism in this sense include Shintoism, Hinduism, and pagan faiths such as folk religions and Neopaganism.

Atheism, as an explicit position, can be either the affirmation of the nonexistence of gods,[27] or the rejection of Theism.[28] It is also defined more broadly as synonymous with any form of nontheism, including the simple absence of belief in deities.[29] Many self-described Atheists are skeptical of all supernatural beings and cite a lack of empirical evidence for the existence of deities. Others argue for Atheism on philosophical, social, or historical grounds. Although many self-described Atheists tend toward secular philosophies such as humanism and naturalism, there is no one ideology or set of behaviors to which all Atheists adhere, and some religions, such as Jainism and Theravada Buddhism, do not require belief in a personal god.

Atheism, a (very) brief overview:

- The term *athéisme* itself was coined in France in the sixteenth century.
- Open admission to positive Atheism in modern times was not made earlier than in the late eighteenth century.

- The spontaneous proposition that there may be no gods after all is likely as old as Theism itself.
- Philosophical Atheist thought appears from the sixth or fifth century BCE, both in Europe and in Asia.
- In western Classical Antiquity, Theism was the fundamental belief that supported the divine right of the state (Polis, later the Roman Empire). Historically, any person who did not believe in any deity supported by the State was fair game to accusations of Atheism, a capital crime.
- Diagoras of Melos (fifth century BCE) is known as the "first Atheist." He blasphemed by making public the Eleusinian Mysteries and discouraged people from being initiated.
- For political reasons, Socrates in Athens (399 BCE) was accused of being "atheos" (refusing to acknowledge the gods recognized by the state). Despite the charges, he claimed inspiration from a divine voice (Daimon).
- Christians in Rome were also considered subversive to the state religion and prosecuted as Atheists.
- In the European Middle Ages, hardly any expression of Atheism is known.
- By the 1770s, Atheism was ceasing to be a dangerous accusation that required denial, and was evolving into a position openly avowed by some.

Belief is the psychological state in which an individual holds a proposition or premise to be true.

Buddhism is both a world religion and a philosophy with distribution throughout the world, and significant variation in beliefs among its adherents. Buddhism is based on the teachings of Gautama Buddha, sometimes known simply as "the Buddha," who lived during the fifth century BCE in ancient India. All traditions recognize the Gautama Buddha as an enlightened teacher who shared his insights in order to help sentient beings end their suffering (see the "Four Noble Truths") in accordance with the laws of Karma by realizing the true nature of phenomena and thereby escaping the cycle of involuntary rebirths known to Buddhists as samsara. A Buddhist is one who takes refuge in the Three Jewels: **Buddha**, *The Enlightened* or *Awakened One;* **Dharma**, *The Teaching* (of Buddha); and **Sangha**, *The Community* (of Buddhists).

Christianity is a monotheistic religion centered on the life and teachings of Jesus of Nazareth as presented in the New Testament. Its followers, known as Christians, believe that Jesus is the begotten Son of God and the Messiah (Christ) prophesied in the Old Testament (the part of Scripture common to Christianity and Judaism). To Christians, Jesus Christ is a teacher, the model of a virtuous life, the revealer of God, and most important the savior of humanity who suffered, died, and was resurrected to bring about salvation from sin. Christians maintain that Jesus ascended into heaven, and most denominations teach that Jesus will return to judge the living and the dead, granting everlasting life to his followers. Christians call the message of Jesus Christ the *Gospel* ("good news") and hence label the written accounts of his ministry as gospels.

Faith is a belief in the trustworthiness of an idea. Formal usage of the word *faith* is usually reserved for concepts of religion, as in theology, where it almost universally refers to a trusting belief in a transcendent reality, or else in a Supreme Being and said being's role in the order of transcendent, spiritual things. Informal usage of the word *faith* can be quite broad and may be used in place of "trust," "belief," or "hope." For example, "faith" can refer to a religion itself or to religion in general.

Hinduism is a religious tradition that originated in the Indian subcontinent. Hinduism is often referred to as **Santana Dharma** by its practitioners, a Sanskrit phrase meaning "the eternal law." Hinduism is often stated to be the "oldest religious tradition" or "oldest living major tradition." It is formed of diverse traditions and types and has no single founder. Hinduism's vast body of scriptures is divided into Śruti ("revealed") and Smriti ("remembered"). These scriptures discuss theology, philosophy, and mythology, and provide information on the practice of dharma (religious living). Hinduism is a diverse system of thought with beliefs spanning monotheism, polytheism,[30] panentheism, pantheism, monism, and atheism. It is sometimes referred to as henotheistic (i.e., involving devotion to a single god while accepting the existence of others), but any such term is an overgeneralization. Most Hindus believe that the spirit or soul—the true "self" of every person, called the *ātman*—is eternal.

Islam is a monotheistic Abrahamic religion originating with the teachings of the Islamic prophet Muhammad, a seventh-century Arab religious and political figure. The word *Islam* means "submission," or the total surrender of oneself to the Islamic conception of God (Allah). An adherent of Islam is known as a Muslim, meaning "one who submits [to God]."

Muslims believe that God revealed the Qur'an to Muhammad, God's final prophet, through the angel Gabriel, and they regard the Qur'an and the Sunnah (words and deeds of Muhammad) as the fundamental sources of Islam. They do not regard Muhammad as the founder of a new religion but as the restorer of the original monotheistic faith of Abraham, Moses, Jesus, and other prophets. Islamic tradition holds that Jews and Christians distorted the revelations God gave to these prophets by either altering the text, introducing a false interpretation, or both.

Jainism, traditionally known as **Jain Dharma / Shraman Dharma**, is an ancient religion of India. Jains have an ancient tradition of scholarship and the highest degree of literacy in India. Jain libraries are India's oldest. Jains believe that all living beings possess a soul, and therefore great care and awareness is required in going about one's business in the world. Jainism is a religion in which all life is considered worthy of respect, and it emphasizes this equality of all life, advocating the protection of even the smallest creatures.

Judaism (derived from the Hebrew word *Yehudah*, "Judah" in Hebrew) is the religion of the Jewish people. Judaism is a monotheistic religion based on principles and ethics embodied in the Hebrew Bible (Tanakh), as further explored and explained in the Talmud and other texts. Judaism is among the oldest religious traditions still being practiced today. In modern Judaism, central authority is not vested in any single person or body but in sacred texts, traditions, and learned Rabbis who interpret those texts and laws. According to Jewish tradition, Judaism begins with the Covenant between God and Abraham (ca. 2000 BCE), the patriarch and progenitor of the Jewish people. Throughout the ages, Judaism has adhered to a number of religious principles, the most important of which is the belief in a single, omniscient, omnipotent, benevolent, transcendent God, who created the universe and continues to govern it.

Pluralism is used, often in different ways, across a wide range of topics to denote a diversity of views, and stands in opposition to one single approach or method of interpretation. **Religious pluralism** is a term used to describe the acceptance of all religious paths as equally valid, promoting coexistence.

A **religion** is a set of tenets and practices, often centered upon specific supernatural and moral claims about reality, the cosmos, and human nature, and often codified as prayer, ritual, or religious law. Religion also encompasses ancestral or cultural traditions, writings, history, and mythology, as well as personal faith and religious experience. The term "religion" refers to both the personal practices related to communal faith and to group rituals and communication stemming from shared conviction.

Spiritualism is a religion founded in part on the writings of the Swedish mystic Emanuel Swedenborg (1688–1772). It is theistic, postulating a belief in God, but the distinguishing feature is belief that spirits of the dead can be contacted, either by individuals or by gifted or trained "mediums," who can provide information about the afterlife.

Spirituality, in a narrow sense, concerns itself with matters of the spirit, a concept closely tied to religious belief and faith, a transcendent reality, or one or more deities. Spirituality is the personal, subjective dimension of religion, particularly that which pertains to liberation or salvation. Spirituality as a way of life concerns itself with aligning the human will and mind with that dimension of life and the universe that is harmonious and ordered. As such, spiritual disciplines (which are often part of an established religious tradition) enjoin practitioners (trainees or disciples) to cultivate those higher potentialities of the human being that are more noble and refined (wisdom and virtue). Accordingly, many spiritual traditions across diverse cultures share similar vocabulary. Terms such as "path," "work," and "practice" are universally applied to the ongoing discipline involved in transforming the coarser energies present in the human soul into more subtle and pleasing ones. As a spiritual practitioner, one seeks to become free of the lesser egoic self (or ego) in favor of being more fully one's "true self."

Theism is defined as a philosophical system that interprets man's worthiness in terms of one God. Thus it is the belief in the existence of one or more divinities or deities. The term itself is interchangeable with *monotheism*. Theism contrasts with nontheism, the state of not believing in deities.

Taoism refers to a variety of related philosophical and religious traditions and concepts. These traditions have influenced East Asia for over two thousand years, and some have spread internationally. The Chinese character *Tao* (or *Dao*, depending on the Romanization scheme) means "path" or "way," although in Chinese religion and philosophy it has taken on more abstract meanings. Taoist propriety and ethics emphasize the Three Jewels of the Tao: compassion, moderation, and humility. Taoist thought focuses on health, longevity, immortality, wu wei (non-action), and spontaneity. Reverence for nature and ancestor spirits is common in popular Taoism. Organized Taoism distinguishes its ritual activity from that of the folk religion, which some professional Taoists (*Daoshi*) view as debased.

NOTES

1. My mom, Angie Britt, recounted this experience to me often over the years. The details of the medical description were reconstructed from research.

2. Proverbs 3:5–6.

3. *Alicia* comes from the Greek and means "wise counselor" or "the truthful one." *B'rit* is the Hebrew-to-English transliteration of the word *covenant*. According to *ancestry.co.uk*, *Britt* is an ethnic name for a Celtic-speaking Briton or a Breton. But my family name was shortened from Brittinger centuries ago and is of uncertain origin.

4. Words and music by Bob Cull. © 1976 Maranatha Music / CCCM Music / ASCAP (Administered by Music Services). All Rights Reserved. Used by Permission.

5. Genesis 1:1.

6. John 14:6.

7. From 1983 to 2000, I was involved first as a student and later as staff with Chi Alpha, a campus ministry that emphasizes global activism and personal discipleship.

8. As Mom was reading this manuscript for accuracy, she mentioned that Dad told her he had stopped attending church because "the pastor demanded that he give all of his pay—fifty cents a day—to the church. Lou countered that tithe meant tenth, not all. When the minister insisted, Lou decided that God wouldn't act that way, so there must not be a God."

9. These stats from Wikipedia referenced data from 2005. Please visit the Web site for updated statistics.

10. These stats from World Christian Encyclopedia are from 2000. When available, please consult the newest edition of WCE for updated statistics.

11. Please see the Appendix for a brief history of Atheism.

12. Dr. Brent Neely adds the following: "When it comes to the idea of commitment to a negative proposition, proving an absolute negative is hard to do. Negative propositions typically leave little to live by." Comment received via email 9/1/2008.

13. Population Reference Bureau, 2008 World Population Data Sheet, *www.prb.org*.

14. From personal correspondence with Glen Davis. Glen directs a ministry to college students at Stanford University. Learn more about him at his blog *www.glenandpaula.com*.

15. *www.pluralism.org/pluralism/what_is_pluralism.php*.

16. *www.cia.gov/library/publications/the-world-factbook/geos/xx.html#* People.

17. My first acquaintance with this term came though the writings of Ravi Zacharias (*www.rzim.org*).

18. Sarah Herman Malcolm. Sarah granted me permission to include this excerpt from her message.

19. Revelation 21:1–4 (NLT).

20. From personal correspondence with Christi Cariker Proctor.

21. From personal correspondence with Shawn Thompson Reeves.

22. Ibid.

23. Dr. Beth Grant, co-founder of Project Rescue (*www.projectrescue.com*).

24. An amusing aside: Exactly ten years after giving this speech, I found myself back in Weslaco, Texas, with the very classmates I had challenged that day. Shawn recounts the experience as follows: "I asked Alicia to say the prayer before dinner at our class's ten-year reunion. I knew it would totally freak people out. I knew Alicia had changed, but my classmates didn't know that little bit of information. They remembered Alicia as she was in high school . . . an Atheist. The

most incredible thing to me was they didn't even recognize Alicia. Alicia's countenance had changed. The hardness was gone and now there was peace. She had a glow about her."

25. Merriam-Webster's New Universal Unabridged Dictionary (Barnes & Noble Publishing, Inc., 2003).

26. These definitions and explanations were taken directly from Wikipedia on September 15, 2008. Please refer to *Wikipedia.com* for updated information and specific citations.

27. The Oxford American Dictionary defines *atheist* as "a person who does not believe in the existence of a god or gods." (New York: Avon Press, 1980.)

28. "Atheism," Encyclopædia Britannica Online, *www.britannica.com/EBchecked/topic/40634/atheism* (accessed April 28, 2007). "Atheism, in general, the critique and denial of metaphysical beliefs in God or spiritual beings. . . . A more adequate characterization of atheism consists in the more complex claim that to be an atheist is to be someone who rejects belief in God for [reasons that depend] on how God is being conceived."

29. Simon Blackburn, The Oxford Dictionary of Philosophy: "Atheism. Either the lack of belief in a god, or the belief that there is none."

30. "Polytheism," Encyclopædia Britannica Online, *www.britannica.com/EBchecked/topic/469156/polytheism* (accessed July 5, 2007).

Puzzle Solution

```
M E A N I N G  J  F  E  A  N  H  O  H
P  T S G N A  K  S  C  R  W  I  B  O  T
Z  E  F  L  X  G  N  O  K  I  O  G  P  X  A
R  N  O  I  T  S  E  U  Q  U  N  E  V  S  P
J  O  U  R  N  E  Y  L  N  Q  D  B  M  C  L
E  I  T  F  N  D  E  O  N  N  E  T  S  I  L
G  T  C  R  B  A  I  A  K  I  R  W  F  A  S
D  R  A  P  A  S  M  N  A  H  Y  E  P  S  T
E  U  F  B  U  E  I  H  G  T  H  K  E  C  L
L  T  A  L  E  H  H  M  I  L  C  A  N  I  H
W  H  L  R  T  D  N  L  V  A  R  O  N  E  D
O  I  E  C  P  F  A  I  T  H  A  G  T  N  P
N  U  N  S  E  E  N  J  A  F  E  S  I  C  B
K  Q  I  N  R  G  O  D  W  P  S  M  K  E  H
```

ANGST	JOURNEY	QUESTION
ASK	KNOWLEDGE	REALITY
BEGIN	LIFE	SCIENCE
DEBATE	LISTEN	SEARCH
FAITH	MEANING	SOUL
HEART	MIND	THINK
HOPE	NAME	TRUTH
ILLUSION	PAIN	WONDER
INQUIRE	PATH	

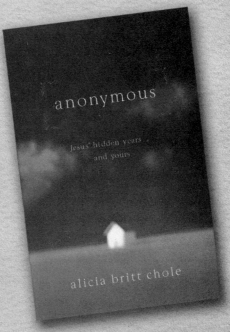